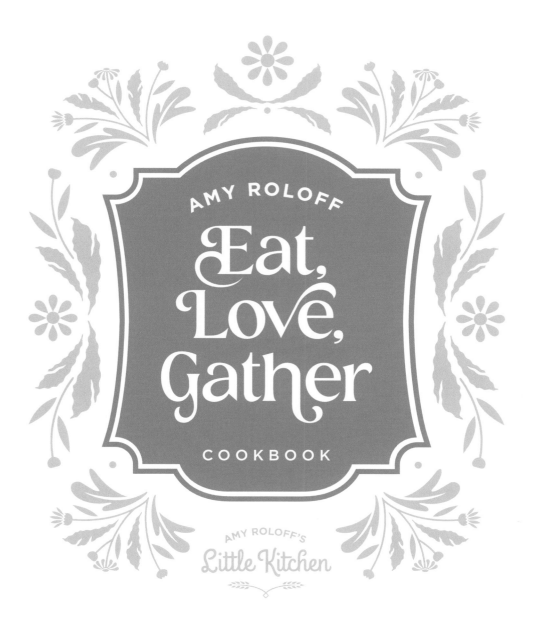

AMY ROLOFF

Eat, Love, Gather

COOKBOOK

AMY ROLOFF'S
Little Kitchen

A Very Special Thank You

To my four kids and all my grandkids who
continue to inspire me and who I love to cook for.

To my family and friends that have gathered
around my table to share a meal and conversation.

To my husband Chris, for loving and encouraging me,
supporting my passions and being my taste tester.

To the chefs and cooks I follow, written cookbooks I've read,
shared their talent, and whom I continue to learn from.

To my parents that started it all by giving me a
play kitchen set when I was a little girl.

To my good friend and business partner, Lisa Dixon, for her
continued support, encouragement and doing so much
behind the scenes to help me do what I love to do.

To my little team, Navid Sanati, Lisa Dorn and Liz Sutton,
that helped me gather the recipes I posted online and
create this cookbook to share with you.

Thank you to All of You for your continued support in
what I love to do, and sharing your thoughts as you have
continued to try my recipes I have shared with you.

I truly appreciate you.

MY interest in cooking, baking and hospitality began when I was a little girl. I remember receiving a play kitchen set for Christmas one year. I would invite my dolls and stuffed animals to join me for meal times. If I did not have the pretend food I needed (such as eggs or bread), I would draw them on paper and cut them out to use. These moments inspired my passion for cooking, baking, and hospitality. Gathering around the table for meals with family, saying grace, and having conversations are some of the most precious memories that I have.

As I became older, I would pour through cookbooks and magazines looking for recipes I could make from my mom's *Better Homes & Gardens* and my *Seventeen* magazines. One of my favorite memories was going to the grocery store with my dad. I loved seeing the variety of foods and ingredients and being able to pick out my favorite cereal (which we usually didn't get to have). Grocery shopping was right up there with clothes shopping. My father was always the faithful taste tester for everything I made. He was a trooper, and he always told me that my food was delicious. He was supportive and encouraging which helped me feel confident to try new recipes. I loved creating recipes, modifying recipes, and experimenting with new combinations and flavors. My mom and dad created a nurturing environment for me to explore my creative side.

I started cooking dinners for my family when I was about fourteen years old. Since both my parents worked full-time, it was often a challenge for my mom to get dinner on the table near dinner time and not late into the evening. When I was asked if I wanted to begin cooking some of the family dinners, I immediately said yes! This was an adventure I was ready to begin. I made weeknight dinners as well as on the weekends. I was still young and enjoyed also hanging out with my friends. I would invite them over so that I could cook for them. As I grew older in college, I often would host my own small gatherings. I found that I loved to entertain. I continued to pour over recipes, read cookbooks, and watch cooking shows to get more experience and knowledge in cooking and baking.

I consider myself a self-taught home cook and baker who is continuously learning. My passion began at an early age, continued while raising my kids, and still continues today at home with Chris and I. Some of my fondest memories are watching my grandmother in the kitchen making her famous noodles and chicken soup, observing my aunt's entertaining style at holiday parties, and helping my mom get dinner ready and baking cookies.

This collection of recipes compiled for you are from my postings on social media, *Amy Roloff's Little Kitchen*, and new ideas just for you. Many of you have requested a book to have all the recipes in one place that you can also take notes. From the beginning to the end, these recipes are comforting, tasty, and family friendly. They remind me of my years growing up, raising my own family on the farm, gathering around the table, and new memories I continue to create. I always have an open seat at the table. This cookbook is my way of sharing my passions of cooking, baking, and hospitality with you. Use the recipes in this cookbook to create more of your own memories of gathering around the table with family, friends, and conversations.

From my little kitchen to yours…Enjoy

Amy Roloff

Table of Contents

Soups & Sides

78

NOTE:
All of the recipes in this book are available on AmyRoloffsLittleKitchen.com.
Some of the images used are taken directly from the videos on the site.
Cook along with me by following the book and the videos!

Baked Goods

118

Entrées

ALBACORE TUNA GRAIN BOWL

What can be better than a power food dish that is made pretty much in one bowl? It's not only good but it's also nutritious for you.

The one thing I love about a grain bowl is you can add in anything you like. The dressing helps to finish the dish as without it, a grain bowl can be a little dry.

Good tuna or other protein, colorful greens, vegetables and a quality grain make up for a good bowl. Some varieties of what I think are good grains: brown rice, quinoa, barley, bulgur and farro. I use rice and quinoa probably the most, but bulgur is very good, too. Also, don't forget the greens, such as spinach and kale.
The vegetables are endless. Go for it, give a grain bowl a try. It's easy to make. What takes the most time is cutting up the vegetables.

I know I'm going to make this or other grain bowls often.

NOTE: This recipe can be easily adjusted for desired servings.

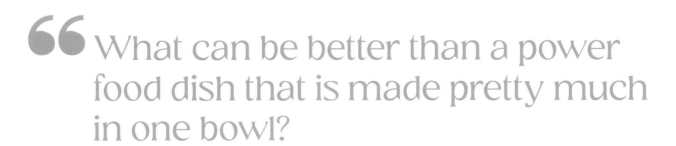

66 What can be better than a power food dish that is made pretty much in one bowl?

INGREDIENTS

1 or 2 cans Albacore Tuna, broken up in large chunks

1-2 Carrots, grated

½ Yellow Pepper, sliced into thin strips

8 Grape or Cherry Tomatoes, cut in half

½ English Cucumber, cut into chunks

2 Radishes, thinly sliced

1 Avocado, thinly sliced

2 Eggs, hard boiled, sliced in half

12 Snow Peas, cut in half

Handful Spinach

1 cup Brown Rice, cooked, *(about ½ cup per bowl)*

Parsley or Cilantro, for garnish

Sesame Seeds, for garnish

DRESSING

2 Tbsp Olive Oil

1 Tbsp Sesame Oil, regular or toasted

1 Tbsp Soy Sauce, or more

2 tsp Red Wine Vinegar

2-3 Cloves Garlic, minced or 1 tsp Garlic Powder

½ tsp Ginger Powder

¼-½ tsp Red Pepper Flakes

Salt and Pepper, to taste

Honey, a drizzle or more

Salt, if desired *(the soy sauce will have salt as well)*

DIRECTIONS

1. Prep all of your vegetables, cut, chop or mince.

2. In a small bowl or jar combine all of the dressing ingredients and shake thoroughly until fully combined.

3. Break up the tuna into large chunks.

4. In two large individual serving bowls, layer the ingredients for each. Rice, spinach, tuna and then place the other vegetables around the tuna.

5. Drizzle the dressing all over the salad. Garnish with parsley or cilantro and sesame seeds.

Notes

SERVINGS: 2

TIME: 15 MINUTES

DIFFICULTY: EASY

COD FISH with FENNEL in WHITE WINE BUTTER SAUCE

Cod is one of the white fish you can really do a lot with. It holds up well, mellow in flavor, flaky, healthy and delicious. If you want a quick meal, depending on how you prepare it, cod is good to have on the menu. Like most fish, try not to overcook it because it will end up being tough and dried out.

Fish is good to have when you are craving a lighter meal option.

NOTE: Serve with rice, polenta, or other favorite side dish. I often serve this fish with rice, sautéed mushrooms, and parsley. Green beans with toasted sliced almonds also work well.

 Healthy and delicious, fish is a good change from other heavier proteins like beef and chicken.

INGREDIENTS

1 large or 2 small Fennel Bulbs, thinly sliced

1 Shallot, finely chopped

4 Cloves Garlic, finely chopped

4-6 Cod Fish Fillets

2 Tbsp Olive Oil, or more

4 Tbsp Butter, melted

Salt and Pepper, to taste

1 ½ Tbsp Parsley, chopped

1 tsp Lemon Zest

4–6 Lemon slices

⅓ cup White Wine

¼ cup Plain Breadcrumbs

¼ cup Panko Breadcrumbs

Dash of Hot Paprika

SERVINGS: 2-3

TIME: 1 HOUR

DIFFICULTY: INTERMEDIATE

DIRECTIONS

1. Preheat oven to 375 degrees.

2. In a shallow baking pan or dish, drizzle a little butter until the bottom of the dish is coated. Salt and pepper each side of the cod fish fillets. Bake for about 10 minutes.

3. While the fish is baking, in a sauté pan add 1 Tbsp of olive oil and heat up. Add fennel, salt and pepper and cook until just before getting tender. Add garlic and shallot and cook until just beginning to brown.

4. In a small bowl add the breadcrumbs, 1 Tbsp of melted butter, lemon zest and ½ tbsp parsley and mix together until the crumbs are moist from the butter.

5. Remove the fish from the oven. Add the fennel shallot mixture and place around the fish, add the lemon slice around the edge of the fish, add remaining melted butter and White Wine. Spoon a tsp or more of the bread crumb mixture on top of the fish. Place back in the oven and cook for about another 15 minutes until fish is just cooked through to the center and breadcrumbs are slightly brown.

6. Garnish with chopped parsley.

Notes

CHICKEN CORDON BLEU

This is one of my favorite dishes. One of the first times I made this was for friends. We had all graduated from high school. I was off to college and two of them had enlisted in the military. I wanted to make a nice meal as a send off to them. The dish turned out great and we had a memorable time reminiscing about high school.

Previously, I made this meal the traditional way. I pounded out the boneless-skinless chicken breast, layered it with thin slices of ham and cheese then rolled it up chicken. Then I dipped each roll in flour, egg wash, and breadcrumbs, cooked it, and topped it with a nice mustard cream sauce.

This time around I wanted to make it a little easier but just as good. I chose to put a sauce on top of the chicken before baking it instead of after.

66 I love Chicken Cordon Bleu. Here's my version making it a little easier and just as good.

INGREDIENTS

4 Chicken Breasts, boneless and skinless

½ cup Flour, for dusting

Salt and Pepper, to taste

2 tsp Garlic Powder

4–8 thin slices Ham
I used Black Forest Ham from the deli

8 slices Provolone or Swiss Cheese

AMY'S SAUCE

4–6 Tbsp Classic Plain Ricotta Cheese

4 tsp Brown Mustard

Pepper

2 tsp Chives, chopped

Dash of Nutmeg, if desired

TRADITIONAL SAUCE

1 ½ Tbsp Butter

1 ½ Tbsp Flour

2 Tbsp Brown Mustard

1 ½ cup Milk

¼ cup Parmesan Cheese, grated

Salt and Pepper, to taste

Dash of Nutmeg

Chives and Parsley, chopped for garnish

SERVINGS: 4-5

TIME: 1 HOUR 15 MINUTES

DIFFICULTY: INTERMEDIATE

DIRECTIONS

1. Preheat oven to 325 degrees.

2. Pound out chicken breasts. This will help to tenderize and make them even in size for cooking. I chose to cut each breast in half because they were large pieces.

3. In a small, shallow baking dish add in the flour, salt, pepper and garlic powder. Mix together.

4. In a large oven proof sauté pan or cast iron pan add olive oil and heat up the pan on medium to high heat.

5. Do not pat chicken dry, keep them slightly moist. Dredge each piece in the flour mixture and place in the hot pan. Cook each breast until a nice golden color, about 5 minutes. Turn the chicken over and cook for about another 5 minutes until done. *Since we pounded out the chicken breast it should not take too long.*

6. Meanwhile, in a small bowl combine the ricotta cheese, brown mustard, pepper and chives. Mix all together until combined.

7. Once chicken has cooled slightly, add a piece of cheese to each one, then add a piece or two of the ham. Add about a teaspoon or more of the cheese-mustard sauce on top of the ham and top with another slice or two of cheese slices.

8. Place the oven proof pan in the oven and bake for about 15 minutes until the cheese has melted and the chicken is heated through.

9. Garnish with chives and parsley.

Continued...

TRADITIONAL SAUCE

1. In a small saucepan, melt the butter, add in flour and cook for about 1 minute or more until the flour just hints at turning color.

2. Slowly add in 1 cup of the milk and mustard and cook until the sauce thickens slightly.

3. Add in the cheese, nutmeg and any additional milk if needed to loosen up the sauce.

4. Cook until the cheese has melted and the sauce is smooth. Taste, add in salt and pepper, if needed. Cook for one more minute.

5. Drizzle the warm sauce over the baked chicken. Garnish with chopped chives and parsley.

Notes

I paired this with Lemon Asparagus and White Rice. If you would like to have a sauce over the Chicken Cordon Bleu I've included a sauce you can make.

Notes

CHICKEN STRIPS

I've made these Chicken Strips I don't know how many times. What makes them so good is both kids and adults love them.They make for a great appetizer with a couple of different dipping sauces to a dinner meal with a side of Mac and Cheese and side salad.

Recently, I had my two grandkids over to hang out with Grandma.and we made this Chicken Strips recipe. Let's just say it was the quietest I heard from them all day. That speaks volumes to their tastiness.

They are quick and easy to make as well.

NOTE: This image is from my video. Follow along if you'd like.

 Chicken strips are so good both kids and adults love them!

INGREDIENTS

4 Chicken Breasts, boneless and skinless

2 Eggs

1 Tbsp Water

1 cup Flour

2 cups Breadcrumbs

½ cup Panko Breadcrumbs

Salt and Pepper, to taste

1 Tbsp Garlic Powder

1 tsp Smoked Paprika

1 Tbsp Butter

Olive Oil

SERVINGS: 2-3

TIME: 1 HOURS 30 MINUTES

DIFFICULTY: INTERMEDIATE

DIRECTIONS

1. Make a prep workstation:
   - In a small shallow dish add flour.
   - In another small shallow dish add the eggs and water, whisk together
   - In a third small shallow dish add breadcrumbs, salt and pepper, garlic powder and smoked paprika, mix well.

2. On a cutting board, use a meat mallet and gently pound the chicken breasts so each piece has a more uniform thickness. Slice the chicken into strips and place on a plate.

3. In a skillet pan, on medium to high heat, melt the butter and olive oil.

4. Begin the assembly line:
   - Using tongs or a fork, dip several of the chicken pieces in the flour, making sure you coat each piece.
   - Then dip into the egg wash.
   - Next, put each piece of chicken into the bread crumb mixture, being sure to coat each piece.

5. Heat a pan on medium-high heat with butter and oil. Add a few pieces of meat at a time. Be sure not to overcrowd the pan with the pieces. *This will help in cooking and browning each piece of chicken evenly.*

6. Cook for 2–4 minutes *(depending on size of each piece)* on both sides or until brown. Using tongs, place the chicken pieces on a plate lined with a paper towel to drain excess oil.

7. Heat oven on the lowest setting and place a plate or dish with the meat in the oven to keep the chicken strips warm until all of the chicken strips are done.

8. Repeat the process until all the chicken pieces are cooked.

A FEW NOTES

- I like cooking with butter because it adds flavor and taste. However, it burns quickly on high heat. Combining oil and butter together slows down the butter from browning and burning too quickly.

- It is best not to crowd your meat when sautéing or frying. Overcrowding causes too much liquid to gather and you end up steaming or simmering your meat instead of browning.

- Make sure the pan is hot enough. If it's not the meat can absorb too much oil, stick to the bottom, or begin to stew in it's own juices.

- Using a meat mallet is either for tenderizing meats or helping the meat to be more even and uniform in size so the meat cooks evenly.

CHICKEN with FENNEL and ROASTED TOMATOES

This is an easy delicious chicken dish to make for a date night, a family dinner, or small gathering with friends.

Sweet roasted tomatoes add bursts of color and flavor, along with a hint of licorice from the fennel, the combination enhances the flavors of the chicken. Croutons offer a little buttery crunch and the salty olives help to balance the dish out.

Enjoy making this for your next gathering.

 Bursts of sweet roasted tomatoes, a hint of licorice, and crunchy butter croutons.

INGREDIENTS

6 bone-in Chicken Thighs, or

4 boneless Chicken Breasts, or
(If skinless dust with flour, see below)

6 Chicken pieces: 2 breasts,
4 thighs or drum sticks

4 Cloves Garlic

Salt and Pepper, to taste

Olive oil

¼ cup Flour
(if using skinless chicken breasts)

1 ½ Tbsp Fennel Seeds

1 ½ Tbsp Coriander Seeds

1 large Lemon

1 tsp Lemon Zest

2 Tbsp Lemon Juice

½ Lemon, sliced

2 Fennel Bulbs, cored and
cut into wedges (save the fennel
fronds, feathery green, part for later)

1–2 cups Grape or Cherry
Tomatoes or 3 Roma
Tomatoes, cut into quarters

2 small to medium Shallots,
sliced

½–1 cup Olives, Green Olives
and/or Kalamata

Baguette, cut into small
cubes, toasted and seasoned
into croutons

FENNEL FRONDS SAUCE

2 cups Arugula, Spinach or
Kale, chopped

SERVINGS: 6

TIME: 1 HOUR 15 MINUTES

DIFFICULTY: EASY

DIRECTIONS

1. Preheat oven to 425 degrees.

2. In a processor or mortar and pestle, crush fennel and coriander seeds, add lemon zest, salt and pepper.

3. Prep chicken. Wash and lightly pat dry, season with fennel seed mixture, reserving some for later. If using boneless, skinless chicken breasts, add fennel seed mixture to flour and dust chicken breasts.

4. In an oven-proof skillet heat 2 Tbsp of olive oil on medium heat. With skin side down, cook chicken until evenly browned, if using chicken breast lightly brown chicken on both sides but do not fully cook. This may take about 15–20 minutes. Remove and place on a plate.

5. While chicken is cooking, prep the remaining ingredients: slice or roughly chop garlic cloves, remove fennel fronds (save for later) down to the bulbs and slice bulbs and shallots, quarter tomatoes, have olives ready in a small bowl and slice ½ of lemon.

6. Cut baguette into bite-size crouton pieces, place in a bowl and drizzle olive oil and lightly add salt and pepper. Set aside.

7. In the same skillet, heat 1 Tbsp olive oil on medium high heat. Add fennel, stirring occasionally until fennel just begins to soften, about 5 minutes. Season with salt and pepper, and remaining crushed fennel and coriander seeds. Remove from heat and add tomatoes and olives to the skillet along with chicken pieces.

8. Transfer oven-proof skillet to oven and roast chicken until cooked thoroughly through, juices run clear, vegetables have caramelized slightly, about 15–20 minutes.

9. While chicken is roasting, finely chop fennel fronds (feather like greens) until you have about ¼ cup or more. In a bowl add juice from ½ of lemon, chopped fennel fronds, salt and pepper and about ¼ cup of olive oil.

10. When chicken is done roasting, remove from oven and add in arugula, kale or spinach and gently mix. Cover with foil. Place seasoned baguette cubes on a baking sheet and roast until just brown.

11. When done, gently stir into chicken dish, and drizzle fennel lemon oil mixture over chicken and serve.

Notes

Notes

CHICKEN PARMESAN, A LITTLE ITALIAN

I've been making this dish for as long as I can remember. When I started my journey in the kitchen, I was so proud of myself because I made something fancy. When I was a young girl, I used a good quality marinara sauce in a jar. I now make my own sauce.

It is not a complicated dish, and oh so delicious! The crispy breading on the chicken, the subtle robust tomato sauce, and gooey cheese on top are comfort food to me.

NOTE: I like serving Chicken Parmesan over spaghetti or fettuccine buttered pasta sprinkled with grated Parmesan cheese and parsley.

 Who doesn't like the crispy breading on the chicken & subtle robust tomato sauce with gooey cheese on top?

INGREDIENTS

2–4 Tbsp Olive Oil

4 Boneless Chicken Breasts

1 cup Flour

1 cup Breadcrumbs
(combo of Plain and Panko or one or the other)

¼ cup Parmesan Cheese, fresh grated

2 Eggs

2 Tbsp Water, or more

Salt and Pepper

1 tsp Garlic

DRESSING

1–2 Tbsp Olive Oil

1 14 oz can Tomatoes
(I use San Marzano Tomatoes)

3 Garlic Cloves, chopped

2 Tbsp Tomato Paste

Salt and Pepper

1 Tbsp Italian Seasoning

1-2 tsp Sugar *(optional; this helps break up the tart acidic taste and balances out the sauce)*

½ Onion, chopped

Fresh Basil, chopped

TOPPINGS

8 Slices Mozzarella or Provolone Cheese

½ cup Parmesan Cheese, grated

Parsley and Basil, chopped

SERVINGS: 4-6

TIME: 1 HOUR 15 MINUTES

DIFFICULTY: INTERMEDIATE

DIRECTIONS

1. Preheat oven to 350 degrees.

2. On a cutting board, place plastic wrap over chicken breasts and pound out each one to the thickness you prefer. *They should be thinner than when you started out.*

3. In 1 baking dish, add eggs and water, whisk until fully blended. In another baking dish add the flour, and in the third baking dish add the breadcrumbs, salt and pepper, garlic and Parmesan cheese, mix until fully combined.

4. Dip each chicken breast into the flour—this helps the egg to stay on the chicken—then into the egg mixture and lastly into the breadcrumb mixture.

5. In a large sauté pan, on medium-high heat, add 2 Tbsp of olive oil. You may need a little more to finish cooking the chicken.

6. Depending on the size of the sauté pan, place two or more chicken breasts in a heated sauté pan and cook until each side is a nice golden brown, about 4–6 minutes. *Don't worry if chicken isn't thoroughly cooked through, it will finish cooking in the oven with the tomato sauce.*

7. In a medium saucepan add 2 Tbsp of olive oil and sauté the onion until soft, about 5 minutes. Add in the garlic and sauté for about a minute more. Add the can of tomatoes, tomato paste, salt and pepper, and Italian seasoning. Cook for about 20 minutes. Add the basil. Taste for flavor, adjust seasonings and add 1–2 tsp of sugar if needed. Continue to cook the sauce for another 10–15 minutes. Using an immersion blender, *(I love this kitchen gadget),* blend the sauce until smooth or the consistency you prefer.

8. If desired, cut each chicken breast in half. *I usually do this to make smaller portions because I find one breast to be too large.*

9. In a large baking dish, add a little sauce on the bottom of the dish. Place each chicken breast in the pan.

10. Add a spoonful or more of the sauce over each piece. Place the baking dish in the oven and bake for about 10–15 minutes, until the sauce starts to bubble.

11. Remove and add a slice or more of cheese over each breast, a spoonful of Parmesan cheese and bake chicken for another 10 minutes until the cheese is bubbly and has melted.

12. Garnish with chopped parsley and basil mixture.

CHICKEN THIGHS with MEDITERRANEAN SPICES and YOGURT DILL SAUCE

I'm finding myself amazed at why I haven't cooked with chicken thighs more. They are so flavorful, good for you and generally easy to prepare. I'm going to try and come up with more interesting and flavorful recipes using chicken thighs.

In this recipe I wanted to find a good combination of Mediterranean warm spices that would go well with chicken thigh meat and the spices in this recipe work perfectly.

I paired the meat with rice, quinoa and lemon. I love cooking with lemon and it seems to be used a lot in Mediterranean cooking as well. Of course any side dish you like will go well with this dish.

 Mediterranean warm spices go well with chicken and the spices in this recipe work perfectly.

INGREDIENTS

4-6 Boneless, Skinless Chicken Thighs (or regular skin bone-in thighs)

3 tsp Salt

½ tsp Pepper

3 tsp Garlic Powder

1 tsp Coriander

1 ½ tsp dried Oregano

1 tsp Cumin

2 tsp Sweet Paprika

½ tsp Allspice

¼–½ tsp Nutmeg, grated

1 tsp Basil

Olive Oil

1 small Lemon, juiced and zested

Parsley, chopped for garnish

YOGURT DILL SAUCE

1 cup Greek Yogurt

¼–⅓ cup fresh Dill, chopped or 2 Tbsp dried Dill

2–3 Garlic Cloves, minced

½ Lemon juiced and zested

Salt to taste

Dash of Hot Paprika

Parsley, chopped for garnish

SERVINGS: 2-3

TIME: 1 HOUR

DIFFICULTY: INTERMEDIATE

DIRECTIONS

1. Preheat oven to 350 degrees.

2. As the meat is cooking, in a small bowl mix together the yogurt, dill, garlic, lemon juice and zest, salt and paprika until all combined. Cover and refrigerate until ready to use.

3. Add all of the spices in a small bowl and mix together. Rub each of the thighs thoroughly with the spice rub. Drizzle with olive oil and the zest and juice of one small lemon. Cover and refrigerate for about 30 minutes.

4. In a sauté pan, on medium high heat, add olive oil. Place the thighs, as many as you can, without crowding, in the pan, along with any juice and cook for about 10 minutes on each side. Cook in batches if needed. Once all of the thighs are cooked add them back into the pan. If not cooked all the way through, place the oven proof sauté pan in the oven for about another 10 minutes until the meat is cooked all the way through.

5. Serve the chicken thighs on a platter with the yogurt sauce on the side and sprinkle parsley over the meat.

Notes

CHICKEN WHITE BEAN CHILI

I like Chili and nothing beats a cold rainy spring day like this comforting White Chicken Bean Chili. It's a wonderful change from the traditional beef and tomato chili.

The creaminess from the white beans and cream cheese gives this chili that rich mellow taste, but it doesn't hide the subtle warm seasonings of chili powder and other seasonings.

I made it easier by using rotisserie chicken. I serve this with corn muffins and a salad. A good hearty bread or chips works well, too.

 Nothing beats a cold, rainy day like this comforting White Chicken Bean Chili.

INGREDIENTS

1 Rotisserie Chicken, meat shredded

2 Tbsp Olive Oil

1 small Onion, chopped

3 Carrots, chopped

2 cans White Beans, drained

1 can White Beans, drained and mashed

4 oz Cream Cheese, softened

1 can Corn, drained (optional)

3-4 Garlic Cloves, chopped

1 Jalapeno Pepper, deseeded and minced

1 tsp Smoked Paprika

2 Tbsp + 1 tsp Chili Powder

2 tsp dried Oregano

2 ½ tsp Cumin

1 tsp Ground Coriander

Salt and Pepper

3 cups Chicken Broth

1 Lime, zested

½ Lime, juiced

3 Tbsp Cilantro, chopped

Serve with shredded Monterey Jack or Provolone Cheese, Sour Cream, Cilantro and Avocado

SERVINGS: 4-6

TIME: 1 HOUR

DIFFICULTY: INTERMEDIATE

DIRECTIONS

1. If you haven't done it yet, shred the chicken.

2. In a large pot, heat olive oil on medium-high heat. Add in the chopped carrots and cook for about 3 minutes. Add in the onions and cook for another 5 minutes. Just before vegetables are done add in the garlic and cook for a minute more.

3. To the pot add in the seasonings, chicken broth, jalapeno pepper and bring to a low boil and reduce heat. Add in the beans and the mashed beans and cream cheese and stir until combined.

4. Add in the shredded chicken and lime juice and stir until all of the ingredients are heated through. This is the time to taste and add in any additional seasonings and salt and pepper. Just before serving add in the cilantro.

5. Serve in bowls with cheese, a little dollop of sour cream and sprinkle of cilantro and a slice or two of avocado. Or have the toppings available for serving.

Notes

CHICKEN with PARMESAN BREADCRUMBS and FETTUCCINE ALFREDO

This is one of my go to recipes because it's simply good and doesn't take a whole lot of time to make.

The crispy crunch of the chicken goes well with the nice pasta and creamy Alfredo sauce. It's just so delicious.

> " This is one of my go to recipes. It's simply good and doesn't take a whole lot of time to make.

INGREDIENTS

4 Chicken Breasts, boneless

Olive Oil *(for sautéing chicken)*

⅓ cup Flour

2 Eggs

1 Tbsp Water

1 cup Panko Breadcrumbs

⅓ cup Parmesan Cheese, grated

Salt and Pepper

1 tsp Garlic Powder

FETTUCCINE ALFREDO

½ pkg Fettuccine Noodles

½ cup Butter *(one stick)*

1 Tbsp Garlic, finely chopped

2 cups Heavy Cream

1 ½ cup Parmesan Cheese, grated

Salt and White Pepper

Dash of Nutmeg, grated *(optional)*

GARNISH: *(Optional)*

Juice of one small Lemon

¼ cup Parsley, chopped

SERVINGS: 4-6

TIME: 1 HOUR

DIFFICULTY: INTERMEDIATE

DIRECTIONS

1. Preheat oven to 350 degrees.

2. Pound each Chicken Breast with the flat side of the meat mallet. You can do this by placing plastic wrap over chicken and pound until flatten to about ¼ –½ inch.

3. Create your flour, egg, & breadcrumb assembly.
   - In a shallow dish combine flour, salt and pepper and garlic powder.
   - In another shallow dish add the eggs and water and mix together.
   - In another shallow dish combine the breadcrumbs and grated Parmesan cheese.

4. Preheat sauté pan with a couple of glugs of olive oil.

5. Dredge each chicken breast into the flour, then egg mixture and then breadcrumbs, patting chicken down into the breadcrumb mixture.

6. Place one or more chicken breasts in the heated pan and cook each side for about 3–5 minutes just until each side is brown. Place on plate. Repeat with the other chicken breasts.

7. In the preheated oven, place chicken breasts in a shallow baking dish and bake for about 10–15 minutes until fully cooked inside.

Continued...

FETTUCCINE ALFREDO

In the meantime, in a saucepan bring water to a boil and add in the fettuccine noodles. Cook for about 10–15 minutes until done and the noodles still have a slight bite to them.

1. In a deep sauté pan, on medium heat melt the butter. Add in the garlic and cook until fragrant. Add in heavy cream and cook until it begins to thicken. Slowly stir the sauce often to prevent it from browning on the bottom and to help the sauce thicken. *This will take a little more time to wait until it thickens but I think it's worth it. It's a lighter Alfredo sauce then when I use flour to help thicken up the sauce.*

2. Add in the Parmesan cheese and keep stirring often until the sauce thickens and is smooth.

3. Add the fettuccine noodles to the sauce *(along with some of the pasta water which will help with flavor and to thicken the sauce)* and slowly mix together until the noodles are coated with the alfredo sauce. Continue to cook until everything is heated through.

4. Place a big spoonful of pasta on a plate, add a chicken breast, squeeze some lemon juice all over and sprinkle with some parsley. If desired, grate a little Parmesan cheese, as well.

Notes

This dinner goes well with a Caesar, green salad, or favorite vegetable.

Notes

FRIED CHICKEN SANDWICH

Ahh… Fried Chicken sandwiches. Who doesn't like a good fried chicken to crunch into?

With crisp lettuce and a good mayo sauce. Or, perhaps you like a little slaw to go with it and most definitely a thin sliced dill pickle. The best!

This sandwich reminds me of summertime. However, frying isn't always my friend or I should say I may have been intimidated by frying. So, I went back to something I like, this chicken sandwich, to give it a whirl again. I'm glad I did. I love the sandwich and hope you do too.

Make it anytime, it's not just for summertime. It's great for a backyard picnic, gathering, or pot luck.

NOTE: This image is from my video. Follow along if you'd like.

66 Who doesn't like a good fried chicken to crunch into?

INGREDIENTS

4 Chicken Breasts, boneless

2 cups Buttermilk

¼ tsp Red Pepper Powder (Cayenne) or about 3-5 drops Tabasco Sauce

½ tsp Garlic Powder

½ tsp Salt

½ tsp Pepper

Vegetable or Canola Oil, for frying

Ciabatta or other Buns

FLOUR DREDGE

1 ½ cups Flour

1 tsp Baking Powder

¼ tsp Red Pepper Powder

½ tsp Garlic Powder

¼ tsp Onion Powder

½ tsp Paprika, smoked or regular

Salt and Pepper

MAYO SAUCE

⅓ cup Mayo

1 Tbsp Apple Cider

Salt and Pepper

½ tsp Hot Paprika Powder

Salt and Pepper

TOPPINGS SUGGESTIONS

Lettuce, Romaine or Iceberg

Dill Pickles, thinly sliced

Tomato

Cheese

Slaw

DIRECTIONS

1. Pound out each chicken breast to even out the thicker part of the breast. If necessary, cut each chicken piece in half if it's too big for the bun.

2. In a shallow baking dish add in the buttermilk, red pepper powder *(or Tabasco sauce)*, garlic powder, salt and pepper.

3. Immerse each chicken breast in the buttermilk mixture and fully cover. Marinate for a couple of hours, up to overnight in the fridge.

4. Before dredging and frying, let the chicken in the marinade come to room temperature for about 15 minutes.

5. Get a heavy duty Dutch oven, cast iron high side sauté pan, or other large pot ready for frying by adding the oil. Turn up to a medium to high heat until it reaches about 350 degrees. *Too high of a heat may burn and fry the outside but may not cook the inside. Be careful of the high heat and possibility of the oil 'spitting' when you put the chicken in, so, stand back at first after placing the meat in the pan.*

6. Dredge the chicken in the flour mixture and once oil is ready, put chicken in the oil. It will take about 4–6 minutes on each side to fry the chicken.

7. Prepare a plate lined with a paper towel or cooling rack with paper towel underneath. Once the chicken is done, place on the rack. Continue until all the chicken pieces are done. *Remember not to overcrowd the frying pan.*

8. In a small bowl, mix together the mayo mixture. And if desired, toast the inside of the buns.

9. Spread the mayo on the bun, add chicken, lettuce and either a pickle on top or on the side of the plate. If making slaw, add slaw on top of the chicken, pickle or on the side.

SERVINGS: 2

TIME: 1 HOUR 30 MINUTES

DIFFICULTY: INTERMEDIATE

Notes

Notes

LEMON PEPPER CHICKEN with LEMON CHIVE PASTA

I love this recipe. It's simple, good, and quick to make. If you don't have a lot of time, give this recipe a try, everyone will love it.

I've made a number of recipes with chicken and lemon in them. The combination of the two is excellent.

I didn't have lemon pepper spice on hand, so I improvised, and made my own. With this you can control the amount of salt and lemon zest, to your liking.

66 I love this recipe. It's simple, good and quick to make.

INGREDIENTS

4 Chicken Breasts

¼ cup Flour

3 Tbsp Lemon Pepper Seasoning

Olive Oil

4 Tbsp Butter

4 Garlic Cloves, minced

1 Lemon, juiced and zested

1 Tbsp Chives, chopped

1 Tbsp Parsley, chopped

Salt and Pepper, as needed

AMY'S LEMON PEPPER SUBSTITUTE

2 Lemons, zested

2 tsps Black Pepper

1 tsp Salt

LEMON CHIVE PARSLEY

8 oz Linguine or
Angel Hair Pasta

1 Lemon, juiced and zested

1–2 Tbsp Chives, chopped

¼ cup Parmesan Cheese

¼ cup Butter

Salt and Pepper to taste

SERVINGS: 4

TIME: 1 HOUR 30 MINUTES

DIFFICULTY: INTERMEDIATE

DIRECTIONS

1. Prep chicken. You can use a meat mallet and pound out each breast until thin or you can use a sharp knife and slice the chicken breast in half and pound if needed.

2. In a baking dish, combine the flour and lemon pepper seasonings *(lemon, zest and pepper)* and mix together.

3. Dredge the chicken pieces in the flour. Heat up a sauté pan or cast iron pan on medium high heat. Drizzle with olive oil. Cook each the chicken breast for about 3–5 minutes on each side. Put the chicken pieces on a clean plate.

4. In the same pan, add the butter until melted. Then add in the lemon zest, juice and garlic. Cook for several minutes. Add in the broth and stir until it comes to a slow boil and reduce. Add in the chicken pieces and finish cooking until warm.

5. Cook the pasta according to package directions or al dente. Drain, reserving about a tablespoon or more of the pasta water.

6. In a bowl add in the butter, lemon juice and zest, stir until mixed in.

7. Plate the pasta and chicken by twirling the pasta and placing on the plate. Add the chicken on top or the side and spoon the sauce over the chicken and sprinkle with the chive and parsley.

Notes

BOLOGNESE SAUCE
with PASTA

I have often made spaghetti sauce, which included meat, onions and herbs, when cooking for my family. It is one of my son's, Zach, favorite. So when I wanted to make a Bolognese sauce I wondered what the difference was. The difference is adding meat and vegetables, like carrots and onions and sometimes celery.

From what I've read, Bolognese sauce is like a Ragú in Italian and made with vegetables and the meat is cooked quickly and often finishes cooking in the sauce. Where Spaghetti sauce is usually just a tomato sauce with herbs.

I'll continue to make a Bolognese sauce because it's good, rich and hearty.

This sauce is just as good if not richer in flavor the next day.

" This sauce is just as good if not richer in flavor the next day.

INGREDIENTS

Olive Oil

1 lb Ground Beef

1/lb Ground Pork

Salt and Pepper

1 small Onion, finely diced

2 Carrots, finely diced

2 Celery, finely diced

2–4 Garlic Cloves, finely chopped

4–6 thin slices Pancetta, chopped

28 oz can + one 14.5 oz Crushed Tomatoes (decrease if you use less than 2 lbs meat above)

1 6 oz can Tomato Paste

1 Tbsp dried Oregano or 2 Tbsp fresh Oregano, chopped

1 Bay Leaf

1 cup good Red Wine

½ cup Chicken Stock

¼–½ cup Cream, if desired

GARNISH

Chiffon, chopped

Basil, chopped

Parsley

Shaved Parmesan Cheese

SERVINGS: 2

TIME: 2 HOURS 30 MINUTES

DIFFICULTY: INTERMEDIATE

DIRECTIONS

1. Prep your vegetables and Pancetta.

2. If using whole San Marzano tomatoes, use an immersion blender to crush and/or chop the tomatoes.

3. In a large deep sauté pan or Dutch oven type pot, cook onions, carrots and celery on medium heat, until just soft. Add in the Pancetta and continue to cook until the Pancetta is slightly crispy. Add in the garlic and continue to cook until soft and aromatic. Remove vegetables and pancetta to a small bowl.

4. In the same pan add in the meat and cook on medium to high heat. Add Salt and Pepper to season the meat.

5. Break up the meat and let it set while cooking. Once brown, flip over the cooked meat to cook the other side until brown. If the meat is not fully cooked, no worries, the meat will continue to cook in the sauce.

6. Add in the red wine to the meat and cook until most of the alcohol has evaporated and the bits of meat left on the pan have been loosened up. Add in the vegetable mixture and stir into the meat. Then add in the crushed tomatoes, tomato paste, oregano and bay leaf.

7. Stir and cook on medium to high heat until it begins to bubble. Then turn down the heat to a simmer.

Notes

BRISKET RUB with BBQ SAUCE

This rub has a good blend of savory and a little sweet flavor to make for a perfect brisket. Brisket is typically an inexpensive cut of meat full of flavor when prepared using this rub.

Your best results will be to use the rub all over the meat and let it set in the refrigerator at least an hour. It's even better for 4-6 hours, or overnight.

A brisket can be sliced for a more elegant presentation or 'pulled' for sandwiches.

This is my version of a perfect rub for a brisket, and other cuts of meat.

NOTE: You can store rub in an airtight container up to four months, until ready to use again.

 This is my version of a perfect rub for a brisket, and other cuts of meat, topped with homemade BBQ sauce.

INGREDIENTS

1 2–5lb Small Brisket, preferably the flat end

⅓ cup Brown Sugar

1 Tbsp Paprika

2 Tbsp Smoked Paprika

2 tsp Black Pepper

1 Tbsp Kosher Salt

1 ½ Tbsp Garlic Powder

1 Tbsp Onion Powder

¾ tsp Mustard Powder

BBQ SAUCE

1 ½ cup Ketchup, (preferably one with no sugar or less sugar)

⅓ cup Apple Cider

4 Tbsp Worcestershire Sauce

⅔ cup Brown Sugar

2 Tbsp Maple Syrup

2 Tbsp Brown or Spicy Brown Mustard

½ Tbsp Smoked Paprika

1 ½ tsp Onion Powder

1 Tbsp Garlic Powder

½ tsp Cumin

¼ cup Water

Few Red Pepper Flakes (if you want a little heat)

SERVINGS: 10-12

TIME: 5 HOURS

DIFFICULTY: INTERMEDIATE

DIRECTIONS

1. Mix all of the ingredients together and stir. Spoon a generous amount of rub on the meat and with your fingers rub the spices all over every part of the surface of the brisket, including any and all crevices.

2. Let your meat rest with the rub for about an hour, if possible. I think it's better to let it rest for 24 hours in the refrigerator. When you are ready to cook the meat, bring it to room temperature for 30 minutes.

3. Since I don't have a smoker, I cooked my brisket in the oven. Preheat the oven to 250 degrees. Place the brisket in a shallow baking dish and cover with foil and bake for about 4 hours, depending on the size and weight of the brisket.

4. If you want to brown your meat first you may want to use the rub after browning. Since it has sugar, it will burn faster than the browning. So add the rub after and place in a shallow baking dish and bake as above.

5. Make BBQ sauce. Place BBQ sauce all over the meat. It's best to use BBQ sauce towards the end of cooking/grilling. If you use it too soon the sugars will burn and the flavor of the sauce won't mingle with the food.

6. Let meat rest for about 15 minutes after taking it out of the oven. Then thinly slice meat on the bias and serve.

BBQ SAUCE

1. In a sauce pan add all of the ingredients and stir to combine. Bring to a low boil then reduce to low. Add additional water if necessary. Cook for about 20–30 minutes until desire thickness.

Notes

CAST IRON STEAK

I love steak when it's cooked right. A little salt and pepper, a quick sear on both sides and then let it rest a few minutes until done. While the steak is still warm, I like to top it off with rosemary butter for extra flavor.

The secret to perfect steak is not to overcook it. I prefer my steak medium rare.

The hardest choice you'll have to make is what kind of steak to cook or grill. The top steaks are probably Fillet, New York, Rib Eye, T-bone or Top Sirloin.

> 66 Steak. The hardest choice you'll have to make is what kind of steak to cook or grill.

INGREDIENTS

2 Steaks, of your choice

Salt

Coarse Pepper

Olive Oil or other high-heat Oil

4 Tbsp Butter, softened

1–2 Tbsp Blue Cheese

Parsley, chopped

ROSEMARY BUTTER

4 Tbsp Butter

1 Tbsp Garlic, minced

2 tsp Rosemary *(or other herb)*

DIRECTIONS

1. Pat dry each steak.
2. Salt and Pepper each steak.
3. In a sauté pan heat pan on medium to high heat.
4. Sear each side of steak for about 5 minutes each.
5. Plate steaks and cover with foil and let rest. Steak will continue to cook for another few minutes to 5 minutes.
6. In a bowl, mix together the butter and the blue cheese.
7. Place a steak on a plate and a tsp of the blue cheese butter. Garnish with parsley.

SERVINGS: 2

TIME: 20 MINUTES

DIFFICULTY: INTERMEDIATE

Notes

MEATLOAF,
the BLUE PLATE SPECIAL

I have fond memories of having meatloaf. I grew up with my mom making meatloaf for dinner. I made it for my family and I continue to do so today.

Meatloaf reminds me of gone days when you had that one great diner you loved to go to all the time and meatloaf would be on the menu as the day's special. Of course, you had to get the special. It also reminds me of small town America.

Meatloaf makes great sandwiches. A good hearty bread, some of the chili sauce, provolone cheese and lettuce. Believe me it's good.

You can experiment with making meatloaf. I have made it in different ways—just depends on what ingredients you want to put in it or have on hand. I have found whatever ingredient you include I would recommend finely chopping them.

NOTE: Go ahead, make meatloaf. It's hearty and good and may even bring you back to a time of fond memories and bygone days.

 Meatloaf reminds me of small town America, and bygone days.

INGREDIENTS

2 lbs lean Ground Beef

½ lbs Ground Pork or Ground Mild Sausage

Salt and Pepper

4 Garlic Cloves, finely chopped or mashed

½ Onion, finely chopped

1 Red Pepper, finely chopped

2 Eggs

½ tsp Smoked Paprika

1 tsp Italian Seasonings

¼ cup Parsley, chopped

1 Tbsp Worcestershire Sauce

¼ cup Parmesan Cheese, grated

¼ Breadcrumbs

¼ cup Panko Breadcrumbs

⅓–½ cup Milk, more or less

CHILI SAUCE

½ cup Ketchup,

¼ cup Pickle Relish

1 Tbsp Apple Cider Vinegar

1 Tbsp Worcestershire Sauce

1 Tbsp Brown Sugar

SERVINGS: 4-6

TIME: 1 HOUR 30 MINUTES

DIFFICULTY: INTERMEDIATE

DIRECTIONS

1. Preheat oven to 375 degrees.

2. In a small bowl add the eggs and with a fork mix until completely broken and mixed well.

3. In a large bowl combine the meat and mix with your hands. I find this a better way to mix instead of with a fork.

4. Add the eggs and mix. Add in the onions, red pepper, garlic, salt and pepper, smoked paprika, parsley, Italian seasonings, Worcestershire sauce, and Parmesan cheese and mix until thoroughly combined.

5. In a small bowl mix together breadcrumbs and the milk until the breadcrumbs have soaked up the milk and are thoroughly combined. Add the breadcrumbs to the meat mixture and mix with your hands.

6. Lightly grease a bread loaf pan to prevent sticking. *Feel free to form the meat by hand into a loaf if desired. I prefer a loaf pan because it helps keep all the ingredients together. Either way will work.*

7. Add the meat mixture into the loaf pan and gently press down and even it out. Run a knife or cake spatula around the edge. *This will help in cooking and to drain, if any, grease after cooking.*

8. Add the chili sauce on top *(optional, I use a good Chili Sauce. I don't want too sweet of topping for the meatloaf).*

9. Bake for about 1 hour and 20–30 minutes. When done, cool slightly before slicing.

10. Serve this meatloaf with mashed potatoes and gravy and a green vegetable or salad.

Notes

MEAT PASTIES,
MY MICHIGAN TRADITION

I grew up in Michigan and I remember making pasties during the cold weather months. They are good anytime of the year. I made them for my kids when they were young and I still make them today.

Think of them like a 'hot pocket'. We call them Pasties. Each time I make them it reminds me of my home state and the history behind them. British immigrant copper minors brought with them these delicious portable meals, for long workdays, in the upper peninsula of Michigan.

They are filling and easy to keep until ready. They are wonderful for road or bike trips, hiking, picnics and camping.

 NOTE: Serve with ketchup or brown gravy and a simple green salad.

66 Pasties are wonderful for road or bike trips, hiking, picnics, camping and more.

INGREDIENTS

1 1lb Ground Beef

2 Rutabagas, chopped in bite-size pieces (or add another potato or two)

2–3 medium Carrots, cut into bite-size pieces

½ large Onion, finely chopped

2–3 small White or Golden Potatoes, cut in bite-size pieces

Salt and Pepper

½ tsp Garlic Powder

½ tsp Thyme

2 Tbsp Parsley, chopped

PASTRY

3 cups Flour

½ tsp Salt

12 Tbsp cold Butter

8–12 Tbsp cold Water

1 Egg (for egg wash)

SERVINGS: 3-4

TIME: 45 MINUTES

DIFFICULTY: INTERMEDIATE

DIRECTIONS

1. Preheat oven to 350 degrees.

2. In a medium sauté pan cook the onions and carrots until slightly soft. Place cooked veggies in a bowl. In the same pan, sauté potatoes and rutabaga until slightly cooked.

3. In another medium sauté pan, brown the ground beef, add in the salt and pepper and garlic and cook until done.

4. In a bowl, combine the ground beef, potatoes, carrots, onions and rutabaga and mix until combined. Add in the thyme and parsley

PASTRY

1. In a bowl or food processor add the flour and salt, mix. Cut in the butter with a pastry cutter or pulse with a food processor until the mixture resembles rough sand.

2. Slowly add in the 8 Tbsp of water until the flour comes together. Add additional water if needed.

3. Combine the flour together and form into a round disk.

4. Place in a bowl and cover with plastic wrap. Refrigerate for about 20–30 minutes.

5. Take out the dough and divide into 6 or more portions.

ASSEMBLY

1. Roll out each disk into a circle. Brush the edge of each circle with egg wash. Take about one big tablespoon of the meat mixture and place in the center of the flour disk. Fold over half of the dough, pinch the edges together and place on a baking sheet lined with parchment paper.

2. Continue to make the other pasties and place on the baking sheet.

3. Brush each pastie with the remaining egg wash and sprinkle with sea salt.

4. Bake in the oven for about 30 minutes until lightly browned.

MONGOLIAN BEEF with VEGETABLES

I love making this dish. It's quick, tasty, and easy to make. It's not too spicy, but I did put a little heat and sweetness into it. When you can combine beef with vegetables, what can't be great about that?

This dish is often made with only beef and broccoli, but I think adding more vegetables enhances the flavor. The sauce coats the beef and dribbles over the vegetables and rice. It's delicious!

NOTE: Beef and vegetables pair well over white or Jasmine rice.

66 Beef combined with vegetables, what can't be great about that?

INGREDIENTS

Olive Oil

1 ½ tsp Ginger, minced

4 Garlic Cloves, minced

½ cup Soy Sauce
(I use low sodium)

2 Tbsp Rice or White Wine
Vinegar

2 Tbsp Water

⅓ cup Brown Sugar
(I use dark brown sugar)

A few Red Pepper flakes
(optional)

1 ½ lbs Skirt or Flank
Steak, thinly sliced
(or another favorite cut of Beef)

¼ cup Corn Starch

½ large Red Pepper, sliced

½ large Onion, thinly sliced

2-3 Carrots, sliced diagonally

1 12-16 oz bag Broccoli or
several stalks Broccoli,
roughly chopped

2 Green Onions, thinly sliced
(for garnish)

SERVINGS: 2-3

TIME: 1 HOUR 30 MINUTES

DIFFICULTY: INTERMEDIATE

DIRECTIONS

1. In a small saucepan, heat oil over medium heat. Sauté garlic and ginger until just fragrant, about a minute or two, but don't let it brown. Slowly add in Soy sauce, vinegar, water and brown sugar.

2. Let it gently boil for about 5-7 minutes until slightly thickened. Add in red pepper flakes, set to a very low simmer.

3. If not already done, prep vegetables and beef and place in separate bowls.

4. In a large sauté pan, heat oil and sauté vegetables starting with the carrots. Add in the onion, red pepper, salt and pepper, cook until just softened and still has a crisp, remove.

5. In the same sauté pan, add in chopped broccoli, salt and pepper and cook until just tender but still has a crisp.

6. Remove and keep vegetables warm.

7. In the bowl with the beef, add cornstarch and combine until all beef is coated.

8. In the same sauté pan as the vegetables, heat oil on medium to high heat, and add the sliced beef. Sear and cook the meat for about 5-10 minutes until done. *The beef does not have to be entirely cooked all the way through as it will continue to cook when combined with the sauce and vegetables.*

9. In the sauté pan with the beef, add in the sauce and cook until bubbly and the sauce has thickened a little more.

10. Add in the vegetables and mix in with the sauce, if desired.

11. Serve the beef and vegetables over white rice and topped with green onions.

Notes

PRIME RIB ROAST

A prime rib cut of beef is one of the best cuts. It has great flavor and is most likely to be more expensive than other cuts of meat. You can get it with the bone in or boneless. Bone in will have a little more flavor, but I prefer boneless. It's easier to cut and slice.

It makes for a great Sunday dinner gathering, celebration or just for the two of you (with left overs).

Serve with your favorite sides and a side of creamy horseradish sauce.

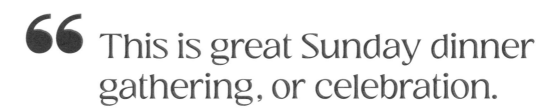

❝ This is great Sunday dinner gathering, or celebration.

INGREDIENTS

1 5 lb bone-in Prime Rib Roast

4 Tbsp Butter, softened

¼ cup Olive Oil

6 Garlic Cloves, minced or
2 Tbsp pre-minced Garlic

6 sprigs fresh Thyme, stems
removed, finely chopped

2 sprigs fresh Rosemary, stems
removed, finely chopped

2 sprigs fresh Oregano, finely
chopped

2 ½ Tbsp Salt

2 tsp crushed Pepper

GRAVY

Roast Drippings

2 Tbsp Flour

1 ¾ cup Beef Broth

SERVINGS: 8-10

TIME: 2 HOURS

DIFFICULTY: INTERMEDIATE

DIRECTIONS

1. Preheat oven to 500 degrees.

2. Sit roast out at room temperature for about 15 minutes, then pat dry.

3. Mix butter and olive oil in bowl.

4. Mix all other seasonings together and then add to butter and olive oil.

5. Rub the seasoning mixture all over roast. Place roast in a roasting pan, fat side up, use the ribs of roast as your rack.

6. Roast prime rib for 15 minutes at 500 degrees.

7. Lower oven temperature to 325 degrees. Continue to roast for about 1 hour or until meat thermometer reaches 120–125 degrees, for medium-rare to medium doneness.

8. Remove roast from oven and cover with foil and let rest for about 20 minutes, this will allow the roast to continue to cook and the juices to mingle throughout the meat before slicing.

GRAVY

1. Pour the roast drippings into a saucepan and cook over medium heat.

2. In a small dish add 2 Tbsp flour and ¼ cup of beef broth. Whisk together to create a paste.

3. Add flour mixture to pan drippings and whisk in and continue on low heat.

4. Slowly add 1½ cups of beef broth to the saucepan while whisking and heating until gravy thickens.

5. Pour over meat and mashed potatoes.

Notes

SALISBURY STEAK, CLASSIC TV DINNER

I remember back in the day growing up and occasionally having TV dinners, it's what we called the 'frozen meal' back then. Even though they were called TV Dinners I wasn't allowed to eat in front of the TV. They were good, convenient, easy and all you had to do was heat them up in the oven, unlike a micro-oven these days, and they were ready.

I remember having them on a Friday night or occasionally on a night when my parents were going out for the evening with friends. Oh yes, having TV dinners do have good memories for me.

I'm going back in time to make one of my favorite TV dinners, Salisbury Steak. Salisbury Steak may seem a little like making meatloaf, but trust me it is different. It's hearty and a comfort food that will satisfy everyone around your dinner table.

NOTE: This image is from my video. Follow along if you'd like.

 Salisbury Steak is a hearty comfort food that will satisfy everyone around your dinner table.

INGREDIENTS

2 lbs lean Ground Beef

⅓ cup Panko Breadcrumbs

2 Tbsp Chili Sauce

1 Tbsp Ground Stone Mustard

½ tsp Salt and Pepper

2 tsp Worcestershire Sauce

Couple splashes Beef Broth
(some will be used for the gravy)

Olive Oil

GRAVY

1 Tbsp Olive Oil

2 cups Beef Broth, or more

½ Sweet Onion, thinly sliced

1 cup Mushrooms, thinly sliced

2 Garlic Cloves, minced

Salt and Pepper

1 Tbsp Worcestershire Sauce

1 tsp Italian Seasoning
(or ½ tsp Rosemary minced)

2 Tbsp Cornstarch or more
(to thicken up gravy)

Couple drops of Seasoning
Sauce, if desired

1 Tbsp Butter

MASHED GARLIC POTATOES

8–12 White or Yellow Potatoes,
cut up in chunks *(or more if
desired)*

½ cup Butter

Salt and Pepper

4–6 Garlic Cloves, minced or
1 Tbsp Garlic Powder

Parsley, finely chopped
(for garnish)

DIRECTIONS

1. For the meat mixture, combine the meat and all of the other ingredients, mix well until all is combined.

2. Form the meat into about 4–6 oval shapes and flatten them slightly.

3. In a large sauté pan, preferably a cast iron, cook steak on one side until brown and slightly crusted. Turn over and cook the other side until done and no longer pink inside. Then set aside.

GRAVY

1. In the same sauté pan, on medium–high heat, add the olive oil. Once the pan is hot add the thinly sliced onions and cook until slightly caramelized and translucent.

2. Add in the mushrooms and cook until just soft and browned. Add the garlic and cook until just aromatic. Remove from the pan.

3. In the same pan reduce heat to medium–low and add the beef broth, Worcestershire sauce, Italian seasonings or rosemary, and heat the gravy until warm.

4. In a small bowl, make a slurry by taking about 3 Tbsp of the beef gravy mixture and the cornstarch and mix until cornstarch is fully dissolved.

5. Add the slurry mixture to the gravy and continue to cook until the gravy has thickened slightly.

6. Add the onion, mushroom and garlic mixture to the gravy and heat through.

7. Add in the seasoning, browning sauce and butter and continue to cook gravy until it comes to a slight boil and has thickened. Turn down the heat.

8. Taste. This is the time to add in salt and pepper, if needed, or beef broth if gravy is thickening up too much.

9. Add the steaks to the gravy, spooning gravy over the meat. Bring the heat down to a simmer and continue until the meat is heated through, for about 5–8 minutes.

Continued...

POTATOES

1. While cooking the steaks, place potatoes in a pot of water, covering potatoes. Cover pot with lid, and bring to a boil. Cook until potatoes are soft.

2. Drain. Add in the butter, salt and pepper and garlic. Mash the potatoes to a consistency you desire. *For this dish I prefer a slightly more fully mashed or creamy textured potatoes.*

3. If needed, add in a tablespoon or more of milk to continue to reach the consistency you want, and any additional salt and pepper.

Serve the Salisbury Steak and Gravy with the steak slightly overlapping the potatoes. A favorite vegetable of mine to serve is green beans, broccoli or a nice green salad

SERVINGS: 8-10

TIME: 2 HOURS

DIFFICULTY: INTERMEDIATE

Notes

I like the Salisbury
Steak with gravy
and good old garlic
mashed potatoes.
It's a perfect meal.

Notes

Notes

Notes

PORK CHOPS with MUSHROOM VODKA SAUCE

This sauce is rich and subtle with a rustic taste of mushrooms that really round out the dish.

When I was coming up with this recipe, a Bloody Mary came to mind. I decided to pair these pork chops with my Bloody Mary salad.

I didn't want to add Vodka directly to the dressing, so I added it to the mushroom sauce so some of the alcohol would cook off.

❝ This sauce is rich and subtle and with the rustic taste of mushrooms.

INGREDIENTS

4 bone-in Pork Chops

Salt and Pepper

¼ cup Butter *(4 Tbsp)*

Olive Oil

1 tsp fresh Rosemary, finely chopped or 1 ½ tsp dried

VODKA SAUCE

6 Tbsp Butter, or more if needed

Olive Oil, about 2 Tbsp.

1 8 oz pkg Mushrooms, Button, Cremini or Shitake, sliced

3-4 Garlic Cloves, minced

¼ cup Chicken Stock, or less

2-4 Tbsp Vodka

Salt and Pepper

2-4 Tbsp Cream

Parsley, chopped for garnish

SERVINGS: 4

TIME: 1 HOUR 15 MINUTES

DIFFICULTY: INTERMEDIATE

Notes

DIRECTIONS

1. Prep all of your ingredients for the meat and sauce.

2. In a large sauce pan or cast iron, heat up butter and olive oil on medium high heat. Season the pork chops with salt and pepper. Sear the chops on both sides, cooking each side for about 5–8 minutes.

3. Add the Rosemary on top of the chops and continue to cook the pork chops reach 145 degrees.

4. Remove Pork Chops and cover and let rest on a platter or in same pan.

VODKA SAUCE

1. In a sauté pan or the same pan, on medium heat, put in the mushroom. Don't add in any salt yet. This pulls the water out from them and will prevent the mushrooms from browning.

2. Cook the mushrooms until they are a nice brown color, for about 10–15 minutes.

3. Turn down the heat to a medium low. Add in the butter, olive oil and garlic and heat until butter has melted and the garlic is aromatic.

4. Add in the Vodka and continue to cook until the alcohol has cooked down.

5. Add in the chicken stock and cream and continue to cook on low to medium low heat until the sauce has thickened.

6. Add in salt and pepper if needed.

7. Plate the Pork Chops and spoon the sauce over them. Garnish with a little Parsley.

PORK LOIN ROAST
with HERBS

This is a simple pork loin roast made with herbs that bring out the pork flavors.

The meat will pair nicely with a number of your favorite side dishes. I've paired it with my Butternut Squash Soup recipe and Spaghetti Squash with Roasted Tomatoes.

NOTE: This pairs well with my red potato salad (page 100) and green beans.

A versatile, simple pork roast that goes with a variety of dishes.

INGREDIENTS

2 ½–3 lb Pork Loin Roast

2 long sprigs Rosemary, finely chopped

2 Tbsp Sage

1 tsp Thyme

1 Tbsp Garlic

1 Tbsp Salt

1 tsp Pepper

¼ cup Olive Oil

DIRECTIONS

1. Preheat the oven to 350 degrees.

2. Blend olive oil and seasonings all together.

3. Rub all over the pork loin roast and let it rest for about 15 minutes before placing it in the oven.

4. Roast Pork for about 2 hours, approximately 20 minutes per pound until meat thermometer temperature reaches 145 degrees.

5. Let rest for about 15 minutes before slicing into serving portions.

6. Use the juices from the meat to make au jus for the pork if you would like.

SERVINGS: 4-6

TIME: 2 HOURS 30 MINUTES

DIFFICULTY: EASY

Notes

PORK LOIN ROAST with a SAVORY RUB

There are a variety of ways to season a pork loin roast. I made another rub using more of what I would call the traditional rub (my Pork Loin Roast recipe). This time though, I wanted something savory that reminded me of grilling my roast on the grill and getting ready for a BBQ.

Depending on the size of your roast, the amount of rub you make will vary, and of course how long you cook it for.

I like the way this turned out and I served it with Red Potato Salad.

I hope you enjoy this rub you can make for your next Pork Loin Roast.

NOTE: I've served this with my Red Potato Salad, page 100, and green beans. It's delicious.

“ I wanted something savory or reminded me of grilling my roast on the grill.

INGREDIENTS

1 ½–2 ½ lb Pork Loin Roast

1 Tbsp + 1 tsp Salt

1 Tbsp Onion Powder

½ tsp Allspice

2 Tbsp or more Garlic Powder

1 tsp Thyme

1 tsp Ground Sage

1 tsp Ground Ginger

1 Tbsp + 1 tsp Smoked Paprika

1 Tbsp Brown Sugar

Olive Oil

MEAT TOPPING

2 Tbsp Tomato Paste

¼ cup Ketchup

1 Tbsp Apple Cider Vinegar, or more

1 Tbsp left-over Rub Seasoning, or more

DIRECTIONS

1. Preheat the oven to 350 degrees.

2. Combine all of the seasonings in a bowl and mix together. Reserving about 1 Tbsp or more for the meat topping.

3. Pat the roast dry. Rub the seasoning rub all over the roast making sure the whole roast is covered. Let it rest for about 5 minutes before searing the meat.

4. In an Dutch oven or straight sided sauté pan, on medium to high heat, add in the olive oil. Sear the roast on all sides and ends to a nice brown color, cooking for about 2 minutes on each side of the roast.

5. In a bowl combine tomato paste, ketchup, vinegar and rub seasoning. Mix together until well combined. Spoon the sauce on top of the roast from end to end.

6. Place the Dutch oven or pan into the preheated oven and cook for about 15 minutes per pound until the internal temp of the roast reaches about 140–145 degrees.

7. Rest the pork for about 15 minutes before slicing.

8. Serve on a platter. If you'd like, spoon some of the juices and drippings from the pan over the meat. Sprinkle the top with chopped cilantro or parsley.

SERVINGS: 2-3

TIME: 1 HOUR

DIFFICULTY: INTERMEDIATE

Notes

GUMBO with SAUSAGE, CHICKEN and SEAFOOD

Let's go southern, or at least a little bit with this traditional southern dish *(think of Louisiana)*. This is my interpretation of Gumbo. Think of it like a stew or soup.

I've learned, by making this dish more than several times, that the main cooking technique to pay attention to is the 'dark roux'. It will take patience and time to get the right consistency and dark color without burning it. The roux is key to the rich flavor which gives you that nice stew-like Gumbo.

The combination of sausage, chicken and seafood is perfect. I used shrimp for seafood but a good hardy white fish will work in this dish as well.

NOTE: Best served with a side of rice.

> 66 The roux is key to the rich flavor which gives you that nice stew-like Gumbo.

INGREDIENTS

2 Tbsp Cajun Seasoning Mix

2 Tbsp Garlic Powder

2 Tbsp Italian Seasoning

2 Tbsp Paprika

1 ½ Tbsp Salt

1 Tbsp Pepper

1 Tbsp Cayenne Pepper

1 Tbsp dried Thyme

1 Tbsp Onion Powder

6-8 cups Chicken Broth

12 oz Andouille or Kielbasa, sliced

Rotisserie Chicken Meat

4 cups Shrimp

4 small Cod fillets or other hearty White Fish, cut into large, bite-size pieces

Your favorite White Rice, cooked, served on the side

SERVINGS: 4-6

TIME: 1 HOUR 30 MINUTES

DIFFICULTY: INTERMEDIATE

Notes

DIRECTIONS

ROUX

1. In a large heavy stock pot combine the flour and oil.

2. Cook on medium-low heat stirring constantly for about 30–45 minutes. Add a little more flour and oil if needed.
    Be careful not to let it burn. Be patient and take the time to cook it and not be rushed, it'll be worth it. The roux should be about the color of light to dark chocolate and have a soft dough like consistency.

MEAT

1. In a skillet brown the sausage or kielbasa until done and place on a plate.

2. Sprinkle Shrimp with salt and pepper and sauté in a pan until just pink.

GUMBO

1. Season the onions, celery and carrots with salt and pepper and cook until slightly cooked.

2. Add 6 cups of chicken broth, the vegetables, tomatoes, Worcestershire and parsley to the pot with the roux and slowly bring to a boil, then simmer. Stir well.

3. Cook for about 10 minutes. Then add the chicken, fish, cooked sausage or kielbasa and shrimp to the pot.

4. Stir in the Cajun seasoning.

5. Simmer for about 20–30 minutes until the chicken is heated through and the fish is cooked. Taste and add additional seasonings if desired and more broth, if needed.

6. Serve in a soup bowl with a spoonful of rice.

JAMBALAYA

Jambalaya is a traditional southern dish. I've made many versions of this in my years of cooking, but for this recipe, I wanted to keep a more traditional southern flare.

Unlike Gumbo, rice is cooked with the dish in a rich tomato base. Creole spices add a depth of rich flavor and a little heat that blends well with the sausage, shrimp and chicken. Let's not forget the nice aromatic flavor of celery, green peppers and onion.

Your family gathering will love their new favorite dish.

NOTE: A nice crusty bread and green salad goes quite well with this dish.

66 Creole spices add a depth of rich flavor and a little heat that blends well with the sausage, shrimp and chicken.

INGREDIENTS

4 Tbsp Cooking Oil

12 oz Andouille or other Spicy Sausage, cut into bite-size pieces

3 boneless Chicken Breasts, cut into bite-size pieces

1 lb medium sized Shrimp, raw

1–3 Tbsp Creole or Cajun Seasoning Mix, depending on your level of heat. *I prefer little heat and more Creole seasoning*

1 tsp Paprika

1 Onion, chopped

1 Green Pepper, chopped

1 Red Pepper, chopped

3 stalks Celery, chopped

3 large Carrots, chopped

4–5 Cloves Garlic, minced

1 28 oz can Diced Tomatoes with juice

1 14 oz can Fire Roasted Tomatoes with juice

Salt to taste

½ tsp Black Pepper

2 tsp dried Thyme

2 tsp Oregano

½ tsp Red Pepper flakes

2 tsp Worcestershire Sauce

1 ½ cups uncooked White Rice

3 cups Chicken Broth, or more

1 bunch Parsley, chopped

Green Onions, chopped

DIRECTIONS

1. Heat 2 Tbsp of oil in a large pot.

2. Season chicken with salt and pepper and a 1 tsp of creole or cajun season. *Omit salt if already added in with seasonings.*

3. On medium heat, brown and cook sausage in a pot, remove with a slotted spoon when done.

4. Add more oil, if needed, and cook and sauté chicken pieces until done, about 6–10 minutes. Remove chicken from the pot.

5. Sauté onions, peppers, carrots, and celery until soft.

6. Add in garlic and cook until soft and blended in with vegetables.

7. Stir in tomatoes. Add in salt, black pepper, cajun/creole seasoning, thyme and oregano, paprika, red pepper flakes, Worcestershire sauce and mix together.

8. Add in cooked chicken, sausage and cook for about 5–10 minutes until heated through, stirring occasionally.

9. Add in chicken broth and rice. Bring everything to a boil, then reduce to low–medium heat and cover with a lid. Simmer for about 30–45 minutes until rice is cooked and liquid is absorbed. Stir occasionally if needed.

10. Place shrimp in the jambalaya mixture, stir gently to incorporate and cover with a lid.

11. Cook for about 6–8 minutes until Shrimp is pink *(cooking time will depend on size of shrimp).*

12. When almost done cooking, taste and adjust seasoning with salt, pepper, and creole/cajun seasonings, if needed.

13. Serve in large bowls and top with parsley and green onions.

Enjoy Gathering around the table.

SERVINGS: 4–6

TIME: 1 HOUR 30 MINUTES

DIFFICULTY: INTERMEDIATE

MUSHROOM 'RAGU' SAUCE
with PASTA

If you need a great recipe to make for a non-meat dinner, I think this is it. I love mushrooms and they are the main ingredient for this rich sauce. There is something 'earthy' and meaty about them and they tend to take on a lot of flavor. Eggplant is another great vegetable you can use instead of mushrooms.

Through my years of cooking I've learned adding salt in the beginning of cooking mushrooms brings out their moisture and instead of browning you end up steaming them. I want to brown them and give them that nice golden color and rustic flavor, so I add salt mid way. Adding salt at the end doesn't give the mushroom a chance to absorb the flavor and they will often taste salty.

Try something different with a nice change from a meat sauce by using mushrooms instead.

 Mushrooms add a wonderful earthy complex flavor that is just as tasty as a meat.

INGREDIENTS

2 Tbsp Oil *(I use Olive Oil but Canola or other will do)*

2 Tbsp Butter

1 small Onion, diced

2–3 medium to large Carrots, chopped

1–2 Celery Stalks, diced

3–4 Garlic Cloves, chopped

1 Tbsp fresh Thyme, chopped or 1 Tbsp Italian Seasonings

16 oz Mushrooms, sliced (2 8 oz pkgs)

4 Tbsp Tomato Paste

½ cup Red Wine, Vegetable Broth, or Beef Broth *(may need more if sauce thickens)*

1 Tbsp Worcestershire Sauce *(or Soy Sauce)*

1 28 oz can San Marzano Tomatoes *(or two cans Fire Roasted Tomatoes)*

1 14 oz can Tomato Sauce

Salt and Pepper

Parmesan Cheese, grated *(optional for garnish)*

Parsley or Basil, roughly chopped *(optional for garnish)*

Linguine, Spaghetti or other preferred Pasta

SERVINGS: 4-6

TIME: 1 HOUR 15 MINUTES

DIFFICULTY: INTERMEDIATE

DIRECTIONS

1. In a saucepan, heat oil on med heat.

2. Add chopped onion, carrots and celery. Cook until just soft.

3. Add garlic. Cook until fragrant. Remove and place in a bowl.

4. In the same saucepan, on med-high to high heat, drizzle just a tad of olive oil. Add in chopped mushrooms. Cook until slightly brown and tender. Add salt and stir. Remove and place in a bowl.

5. In the same cooking pan add in the tomatoes, tomato paste and seasonings. Cook until tomatoes are soft enough to crush, about 15 minutes. *If not using San Marzano tomatoes, then use the two cans of tomatoes and seasonings.*

6. Add in vegetables, seasonings and wine and cook on med-high until the wine has evaporated by half. If not using wine, add in beef or veggie broth and cook until heated through.

7. Add in Worcestershire sauce. Stir and continue to cook on low until all the flavors have come together, about 30 minutes. If you have the time, cook on low for an additional 30 minutes for the flavors to further develop.

8. Taste and adjust for any additional seasonings, garlic and salt and pepper.

9. When sauce is near finished cooking, heat a large stockpot of water and add salt. When water comes to a boil add pasta and cook according to package directions. Reserve ¼ cup of pasta water to add to sauce if needed.

10. Serve Mushroom Ragu Sauce over pasta and sprinkle with Parmesan cheese, parsley or basil or both.

Notes

SIMPLE GRILLED CHEESE SANDWICH

A true childhood favorite of mine and still is every time I make these. Nothing pairs better with tomato soup than a Simple Grilled Cheese Sandwich. I can't resist these nice triangle cut sandwiches, with the gooey cheese, dipped in soup.

There are several cheeses that melt nicely to make your favorite grilled cheese sandwich besides cheddar. Try Colby, Gruyere, Provolone or Swiss, or a combo of any two.

It best to use a good white bread that will hold up to all the goodness and not be too squishy.

Grilled Cheese isn't just for a childhood memory but for grown-ups, too.

NOTE: Goes great with my Rustic Tomato Soup, page 92.

> 66 I can't resist the nice triangle cut sandwiches, with the gooey cheese, dipped in soup.

INGREDIENTS

8 slices hearty White Bread *(or bread of choice)*

6-8 slices Cheddar Cheese *(to cover the whole slice of bread)*

Butter, softened

SERVINGS: 4

TIME: 15 MINUTES

DIFFICULTY: EASY

DIRECTIONS

1. Preheat the oven on low broil.

2. Butter 4 slices bread on one side.

3. Place enough cheese to cover each unbuttered side of 4 slices of bread.

4. Butter the other 4 slices of bread on one side and place the unbuttered side on top of cheese.

5. Place each sandwich on a baking sheet and toast until just brown and cheese has begun to melt. Open the oven and gently flip sandwiches, broil the other side until just brown and toasted and cheese has melted.

6. Serve warm with Rustic Tomato Soup and a dill pickle or other preference.

Notes

Notes

Notes

Soups
& Sides

BUTTERNUT SQUASH SOUP

When the temperature outside starts falling and the leaves start changing, it's time to head into my Little Kitchen and make a hearty batch of soup. What's better than the comfort of a warm bowl of soup on a chilly autumn day? Not much, except for time spent with the people I love.

66 What's better than the comfort of a warm bowl of soup on a chilly autumn day?

INGREDIENTS

3 medium size Butternut Squash

2 ½ box *(48 oz each)* Chicken Broth

4 large Carrots

1 Onion

3 stalks Celery

1 tsp grated Ginger or
1 ½ tsp Ginger Powder

1 tsp Nutmeg

1 Tbsp Salt

2 tsp Pepper

2 tsp Garlic

1 cup Cream

1 Tbsp Lemon Juice

Toasted Pumpkin Seeds

SERVINGS: 10

TIME: 1 HOUR 30 MINUTES

DIFFICULTY: EASY

DIRECTIONS

1. Preheat oven to 425 degrees.

2. Cut butternut squash in half, length wise. Scoop out pulp and seeds. Use peeler to peel outer skin off on each squash half.

3. Cut and dice each butternut squash in bite-size pieces and place in shallow baking pan. Drizzle olive oil and sprinkle salt and pepper over cut up squash and mix together. Roast for about 25–35 minutes until tender.

4. While butternut squash is cooking, dice up carrots, onion and celery.

5. Drizzle olive oil into a heated up sauté pan. Place cut up carrots in pan and add salt and pepper and cook until tender, remove.

6. In same sauté pan drizzle olive oil and add diced onion and add salt and pepper and sauté until tender and translucent, remove.

7. In same sauté pan drizzle olive oil and add celery and sprinkle salt and pepper over celery and cook until tender, remove.

8. When butternut squash has finished roasting in the oven remove and cool slightly.

9. In a large stock pot add squash, chicken broth, vegetables and seasonings. Bring to a boil and then turn heat down to a simmer and cook until squash is tender and can be blended.

10. Once squash is cooked use an immersion blender to blend all of the ingredients into a smooth consistency. Add more chicken broth if the soup is still a little thick.

11. Add cream and keep simmering on the stove. Taste for seasoning and adjust as needed. Taste again.

12. Add lemon juice. It's amazing how this gives the soup a pick me up and brightens it up in taste.

13. Toast pumpkin seeds in a sauté pan until slightly brown and add as a garnish.

CHICKEN TORTILLA SOUP

This soup reminds me of a combination of some of my favorite dishes like tacos and enchiladas.

This is a simple soup to make. Using rotisserie chicken is an easy way to cut down the cooking time. Enchance the dish with a mixture of garnishes such as sour cream, green onions and cilantro.

NOTE: This image is from my video. Follow along if you'd like.

 This reminds me of a combination of some of my favorite dishes, like taco and enchiladas.

INGREDIENTS

3 Tbsp Olive Oil

1 Carrot, chopped

1 Sweet Onion, chopped

1 Red Pepper, chopped

1 Green Pepper, chopped

2 Tbsp Garlic, finely chopped

1–2 Jalapenos, finely diced
(depending on your heat preference)

6 cups Chicken Broth

2 14.5 oz cans Fire Roasted
Tomatoes

3 Tbsp Tomato Paste

2 14.5 oz cans Black Beans,
drained

1 14.5 oz can Corn, drained

2–3 Chicken Breasts or
1 Rotisserie Chicken
(a perfect substitution, as well)

3 Tbsp Seasonings Mix*
(more or less, if desired)

1 tsp Lime Zest

½ Lime, juiced

Salt and Pepper to taste

SEASONING MIX

1 Tbsp Cayenne Pepper

2 Tbsp Chili Powder

1 Tbsp Cumin Powder

1 Tbsp Garlic Powder

1 Tbsp Salt

1 tsp Pepper

2 tsp Oregano

SERVINGS: 4-6

TIME: 1 HOUR

DIFFICULTY: EASY

DIRECTIONS

1. Preheat the oven to 375 degrees.

2. Line a baking sheet with parchment paper. Drizzle about 1 Tbsp oil over chicken and massage chicken until oil covers chicken.

3. Add 1 Tbsp seasoning mix and coat chicken breast with mix. Bake in oven for about 15–20 minutes until center is cooked. Remove and cool until able to shred chicken. If using Rotisserie Chicken, shred chicken and set aside.

4. In a stock pot or large sauce pan add 2 Tbsp oil on medium heat. Add chopped carrots and sauté for about 2 minutes, then add in onion, red pepper, green pepper, garlic and jalapeno pepper and 1 tsp salt and sauté for about another 2 minutes, until the vegetables are no longer raw and cooked slightly but not soft.

5. Add 2 cups of chicken broth, the tomatoes, tomato paste and seasonings to the pot of sauté vegetables and stir until all ingredients are mixed together.

6. Add the remainder of the broth and cook on medium to low heat for about 5 minutes.

7. Shred the chicken breasts and add shredded chicken, black beans and corn to the broth and cook for about 30 minutes until all the ingredients are heated through and the flavors have been incorporated.

8. Taste and add additional salt, pepper and seasoning mix, if needed.

GARNISHES

- Sour Cream
- Cilantro
- Avocado
- 2 Flour Tortillas, cut in strips and baked until just turning golden color
- 1 ½ cups shredded Monterey or Cheddar Cheese
- Red onion finely chopped or 2 Green Onions chopped
- White Rice *(if you want to serve soup over it)*

GROUND BEEF VEGETABLE SOUP

This is an easy comforting soup to make on a cold day. Most of the ingredients you'll probably have on hand.

The combination of ingredients that are put together in this soup is just amazing. It's different than a beef or minestrone soup, and like other soups you can easily make it your own.

Maybe it's just that extra touch of homemade goodness in it. It's fulfilling, quick to make and just so good. Why not make it tonight?

This is great with good crusty bread, or biscuits.

NOTE: This is made in one pot for less clean up and pairs well with biscuits.

" This soup has an extra touch of homemade goodness.

INGREDIENTS

1–3 Tbsp Olive Oil or Butter

1 ½–2 lbs lean Ground Beef *(I used 90/10)*

Salt and Pepper

4–6 Garlic Cloves, minced

1 small Sweet Onion, chopped

2–3 Celery stalks, chopped

3–4 Carrots, chopped

½ tsp fresh Rosemary, chopped *(or ½ tsp dried Rosemary)*

1 tsp fresh Thyme, chopped *(or ½ tsp dried Thyme)* or

1 Tbsp Italian Seasoning, or more

4–6 cups Beef or Vegetable Broth

1 14.5 oz can Fire Roasted Tomatoes

4 oz can Tomato Paste

6-8 White, Gold or Yukon Potatoes, diced into bite-size pieces

1 cup Green Beans *(fresh or frozen)*

1 bunch Spinach or Kale

Dash of Sugar

1 tsp Lemon Zest

1 Tbsp Lemon Juice

½ tsp Thyme

Parsley, chopped for garnish

SERVINGS: 4–6

TIME: 1 HOUR

DIFFICULTY: INTERMEDIATE

DIRECTIONS

1. Heat oil or butter in a large pot on medium to high heat. Add in the carrots, celery and onions. Cook until just tender. Before removing, add in the garlic and cook until fragrant. Remove and place in a bowl.

2. In the same pot, add more oil or butter if needed. Add salt and pepper to the meat and cook, breaking up the meat *(it's ok if there are chunks of the meat)* and cook until just done. Since it's lean meat, don't overcook it or it may be dry. *If using meat with a higher fat content, be sure to drain before adding in other ingredients. Alternative; substitute with ground turkey or chicken.*

3. Add in the seasonings and tomato paste, stir until combined.

4. Add in the broth, vegetables *(except the beans and spinach or kale)*, tomatoes and potatoes into the pot with the meat, and stir all of the ingredients together.

5. Bring the soup to a low boil and reduce to a simmer and cook for about 30 minutes until the potatoes are tender.

6. Add in the lemon zest and juice and stir. Cook for another 10 minutes. Add in sugar, taste. Add additional salt and pepper and seasonings, if needed.

7. Add in the green beans and spinach or kale and cook for another 10–15 minutes.

8. Serve in bowls and garnish with parsley if desired.

Notes

HAM and WHITE BEAN SOUP

I love making soups because you can really make it your own.

I think it is better to use leftover ham, bone-in ham, or ham hocks. It adds is so much more flavor if you do. However, if you don't have this type of ham, using sliced ham from the meat market works well, too.

I often add a little smoked paprika to give it that rustic hint of smoky flavor. Using bone-in or ham hocks may take a little longer to cook to blend the flavors together, but it is well worth it.

I usually use whatever kind of white beans I have in the pantry. Adding in spinach or kale and carrots adds a bright color and softness which are great additions to the hearty soup.

NOTE: This image is from my video. Follow along if you'd like.

66 I love a soup chock full of wonderful fresh ingredients and protein.

INGREDIENTS

2–3 Smoked Ham Hocks or,
1 Bone-in Ham or,
6–8 thick slices Ham

3 strips Bacon, cooked and chopped

2 cans White Beans
(Cannellini, Great Northern, Navy or any other you preferred) or

1 lb dried White Beans, soaked overnight in cold water

2 Tbsp Olive Oil

3 Carrots, peeled and chopped into bite-size pieces

½ Sweet Onion, chopped into bite-size pieces

3 Celery stalks, chopped into bite-size pieces

3 Garlic Cloves, peeled and minced

Small bunch Thyme or
1 Tbsp dried Thyme

½ Tbsp dried Oregano

½ tsp Cumin

½ tsp Smoked Paprika *(if desired and if you're not using Ham Hocks or Bone-in Ham)*

6 cups Chicken Broth, or other preferred Broth

1 large bunch Spinach or chopped Kale, removed from stems

Salt and Pepper, to taste

Parmesan Cheese, grated

SERVINGS: 4-6

TIME: 1 HOUR

DIFFICULTY: INTERMEDIATE

DIRECTIONS

1. In a large stock pot, heat oil over medium-high heat and add in carrots, onions and celery and cook until just heated through but not fully cooked, about 5 minutes, stir.

2. Add ham, garlic and cook additional 3 minutes on medium low heat and stir.

3. Add beans, herbs and spices and broth and mix all the ingredients together and continue to cook on medium to low heat.

4. Cook soup for about 1–1 ½ hours until vegetables and beans are tender but not mushy and meat falls apart.

5. Remove bone and any other fat, skin or other pieces.
   Or remove ham bone and when cool to the touch pull meat apart from bone into cut into bite-size pieces.

6. Add ham back into the pot and cook for another 10 minutes until heated through. Add in spinach or kale and cook until heated through. Salt and pepper to taste.

7. Ladle soup in bowls and sprinkle Parmesan cheese on top, if desired.

Notes

LENTIL SAUSAGE and KALE SOUP

Lentils provide protein, cook up easily and pair well with sausage and kale.

You want to add kale towards the end of the soup simmering. This will give time for the kale to breakdown and soften up.

This soup is comforting and full of flavor. Freshly shaved Parmesan melts over the top. A fresh roll is perfect for soaking up this soup.

 **This soup is comforting and full of flavor.**

INGREDIENTS

2 cups Lentils

1 large Onion, chopped

3 large Carrots, chopped

3 stalks Celery, chopped

3 Tbsp Olive Oil

1 ½ lbs bulk Italian
Sausage or,
1 lb Kielbasa, cut into thick
slices or,
Italian Sausage, casting
removed and sliced

Salt and Pepper

3 large Cloves Garlic, minced

2 Bay Leaves

1 ½ Tbsp Thyme

1 tsp Cumin

1 tsp Rosemary

8 cups Chicken Broth

2 Tbsp Tomato Paste

4 cups Kale, stems removed

½ cup Parsley, chopped

Parmesan Cheese, shaved

Optional: ¼ cup Red Wine or
2 Tbsp Red Wine Vinegar

SERVINGS: 4-6

TIME: 50 MINUTES

DIFFICULTY: EASY

DIRECTIONS

1. In a medium size bowl add lentils and 2 cups of boiling water. Let sit for about 20 minutes and drain any water that is left over. *I like this step because it begins to get the lentils ready and softens them up just a tad before adding to the soup.*

2. Tear kale from their stem and into bite-size pieces into a bowl and drizzle with olive oil and sprinkle salt and gently mix.

3. In a large medium stock pot heat up 1 Tbsp of olive oil and sauté onions, carrots and celery, salt and ground pepper for about 10 minutes until just tender.

4. Add in 1 Tbsp olive oil *(if needed)*, sausage broken up into bite-size pieces, garlic and thyme, rosemary, bay leaf, and cumin, and cook for another 10 minutes or longer until sausage is cooked through.

5. Add the chicken broth, tomato paste and the drained lentils. Bring to a boil and then reduce the heat to a simmer and cook for about 1 hour until lentils are cooked through and tender.

6. Add kale and cook for another 10 minutes or so. Add salt and ground pepper or other seasonings if needed.

7. Serve in bowls sprinkled with parsley and shaved Parmesan cheese.

Notes

RUSTIC TOMATO SOUP

Yum! I love a good comforting soup on a cold night. There is nothing like pairing this tomato soup with an ooey gooey grilled cheese sandwich!

 Nothing says comfort like tomato soup.

INGREDIENTS

4 28 oz cans Whole Tomatoes
(I like San Marzano Style tomatoes)

3 oz Tomato Paste

4 Cloves Garlic, chopped
(or 3 Tbsp minced garlic)

1 small Sweet Onion, chopped

4 Carrots, chopped

Red Pepper flakes

1 Tbsp Brown Sugar*

2 Tbsp fresh Thyme

2 Tbsp Olive Oil

1 Tbsp Butter

Salt and Pepper to taste

1 small bunch fresh Basil,
(rough chopped)

1 small bunch Parsley

3 cups Vegetable or
Chicken stock *(more if needed)*

1 Tbsp Lemon Zest

Juice from ½ a Lemon

3 oz Cream Cheese,
softened**

OPTIONAL

*Brown Sugar softens and mellows out the acidity of the soup and adds a richness to it. White Sugar works well, too.

** Cream Cheese mellows the acidity of the soup and makes it creamy. Add to soup and stir until smooth or use ½ cup Half and Half.

SERVINGS: 4-6

TIME: 1 HOUR 15 MINUTES

DIFFICULTY: EASY

DIRECTIONS

1. In a large stockpot, heat the olive oil and butter over medium-low heat until butter melts. Add onion, carrots, a dash of salt and pepper and cook vegetables until just tender.

2. Add in tomato paste and chopped garlic and cook until blended and the garlic is soft.

3. Add the tomatoes with juice, broth, thyme, a few red pepper flakes, and sugar. Cook tomatoes on medium-high heat, *(don't allow to boil)* until they have broken down and are soft, about 40 minutes.

4. Use an immersion blender and blend until smooth. Add more broth if it is too thick. *I like immersion blender best, less messy and less time it takes to blend the soup until smooth in a regular blender. Don't worry if there are little bits of tomato or other vegetables in soup (it's rustic), unless you like it completely smooth.*

5. Add lemon zest and juice. *Lemon adds a freshness and spark to the soup.*

6. Add cream cheese.

7. Reheat soup on medium low heat until cheese has melted and blended in with soup.

8. Serve warm. Garnish with basil/parsley mixture or any of the other garnishes or other preferences.

GARNISH SUGGESTIONS

- **Croutons**—Cut up bread of choice into crouton bite-sizes, drizzle with olive oil, add salt and pepper and Parmesan cheese and toss. Bake in the oven until toasted and crunchy. Sprinkle soup with croutons, finely cut up basil and Parmesan cheese.

- **Sour Cream**—Mix sour cream with finely chopped basil and/or chives and add a dollop of sour cream to each bowl of soup.

- **Bacon & Chives**—Cook bacon until just crispy, chop until fine. Chop chives. Garnish soup with bacon and chives.

SPLIT PEA with HAM SOUP

Split Pea soup has always been one of my favorites. It's smooth, creamy and so good. It's lightly seasoned with garlic, bay leaf and oregano.

Now add in the Ham and the soup has just elevated. The ham really adds flavor. You can omit the ham and chicken stock and add vegetable stock instead if you want to make it vegetarian.

Enjoy this soup that is very tasty, smooth, and full of flavor for your next meal.

NOTE: This image is from my video. Follow along if you'd like.

 Split Pea soup has always been one of my favorites. It's smooth and creamy and so good.

INGREDIENTS

3–4 Ham Hocks or Shanks,
or leftover Ham
(either will create flavor for the soup)

1 16 oz bag dried Split Peas,
rinsed and sorted

6–8 cups Chicken Broth
(or Vegetable Stock)

2 cups Water, from the
cooked Ham Shanks or Hocks

1 Sweet Onion, chopped

4 Carrots, chopped

3 Celery, chopped

1 Bay Leaf

2 tsp Thyme

Salt and Pepper

3 Cloves Garlic, minced

OPTIONAL TOPPINGS

Croutons

Parmesan Cheese, grated

Parsley

SERVINGS: 2–3

TIME: 5 HOURS

DIFFICULTY: INTERMEDIATE

DIRECTIONS

1. In a large pot place the ham shanks or hocks. Add in enough water to cover them. Add in salt, pepper and garlic to create flavor. Cook for about 2 hours. Cool down until able to handle and cut the meat off from the bones. Reserve about 2 cups of the ham broth. *If using left over ham, skip step one.*

2. In a large stock pot, add the 6 cups of chicken broth, peas, thyme and bay leaf. If you cooked the ham hocks, add in about 2 cups of reserve ham broth. Cook until the peas are just tender.

3. While the peas are cooking, saute the carrots, onions and celery until tender. Add in the garlic and cook until aromatic. Add the vegetables to the split pea broth. Continue to cook until the soup thickens. Add additional broth if needed. Add the ham to the soup and continue to cook for about another 20 minutes until the meat is heated through.

4. Serve with croutons, grated Parmesan cheese and/or chopped parsley and good bread.

Notes

BLOODY MARY SALAD

I paired this salad with my Pork Chops with Butter Vodka Mushroom Sauce.

I'm not sure why or how I came up with this combination of a salad and dressing, but I did. I don't particularly drink Bloody Marys but I wanted to come up with something different for cooking Pork Chops and this salad came to me.

It's crisp and I like the combo of tomatoes, red onions and celery with a dressing that reminds me of a Bloody Mary.

> ❝ I like the combo of tomatoes, red onions and celery with a dressing that reminds me of a Bloody Mary.

INGREDIENTS

One head Romaine Lettuce, chopped

Roma or Cherry Tomatoes, cut in quarters or halves

1 Celery stalk, with leaves, sliced and leaves chopped.

½ half (or less) Red Onion, thinly sliced

Parsley, chopped

DRESSING

¼ cup Olive Oil

1–2 Tbsp Red Wine Vinegar

1 tsp Lemon Zest and Juice

Salt and Pepper

2 tsp Worcestershire Sauce

¼ tsp Horseradish Sauce

Couple dashes Tabasco or Sriracha Sauce

SERVINGS: 2

TIME: 15 MINUTES

DIFFICULTY: EASY

DIRECTIONS

1. Prep your vegetables; chop the romaine lettuce. Cut up tomatoes, celery stalk and leaves and slice red onion.

2. Plate on individual serving plates starting with romaine lettuce and then the remaining ingredients.

3. In a small bowl, combine all of the dressing ingredients and stir well until thoroughly combined. Taste and add in any additional ingredients if needed.

4. Drizzle over salad, garnish with parsley, and serve.

Notes

GREEN SALAD

One day I was looking in my fridge to see what I had to make a salad for dinner and all I saw was a lot of green. I had lots of green goodness in my fridge. So I decided to make what I call a 'green salad'. Everything in the salad had to be green, no tomatoes, unless they were green. I hoped what I saw in my fridge would be enough to make a good and healthy salad.

To really taste the different textures and variety from all the greens I decided that a simple vinaigrette dressing would go great with it. I didn't want to cover all of the deliciousness with a heavy dressing.

This is a perfect salad to make in your own way. So take a look in your fridge and see what is (good) green and would make for a good in a salad. You'll end up with a great salad too.

There are so many different things you can put in your bowl that's green. Here's an idea of items I have put in my Green Salad. Not all at once, it just depends on what I have in my fridge and the mood I'm in.

NOTE: I usually just add three or maybe four veggies at the most, depending on what the veggie is. I think too heavy on the veggies can crush and weigh the greens down.

66 All About the 'power' of green...
Green Salad that is.

GREEN SUGGESTIONS

The Greens:

Leaf Lettuce	Arugula
Romaine	Iceberg
Spinach	Kale

The Veggies:

Brussels Sprouts	Snow Peas
Green Onions	Broccoli
Peas	Zucchini
Green Olives	Avocado

Asparagus *(par cooked)*
Green Beans *(par cooked)*
Cucumber *(I prefer English)*

The Herbs:

Chives	Thyme
Parsley	Basil
Cilantro	Dill

The Fruit:

Grapes
Kiwi
Green Apple

The Nuts:

Pistachios
Walnuts *(not green but sometimes you have to go outside the box)*

The Cheese:

Ok, it's not green but ... I love cheese, I usually use shaved Parmesan.

VINAIGRETTE

½ cup Olive Oil

¼ cup Champagne Vinegar or White Wine Vinegar

1 ½ Tbsp Lemon Juice*

1 tsp Garlic

Salt and Pepper to taste

Variation—Instead of Lemon Juice, use 1 tsp Dijon Mustard

DIRECTIONS

1. Prep your vegetables. Chop the Romaine Lettuce, cup up tomatoes, celery stalk and leaves and slice red onion.

2. Plate on individual serving plates starting with romaine lettuce and then the remaining ingredients.

3. In a small bowl, combine all of the dressing ingredients and stir well until thoroughly combined. Taste and add in any additional ingredients if needed.

4. Drizzle over salad garnish with parsley, and serve.

VINAIGRETTE

Combine all ingredients in a small bowl or jar and whisk or shake until mixed well.

Here's an example of a combo I have put together from my fridge. The size of the salad depends on the number of people you are serving.

GREENS: Romaine, leaf (purple and green) lettuce, spinach and arugula.

VEGGIES: Green onions, green beans (par cooked and cooled), (about) 4 brussels sprouts, and 1 small zucchini.

HERBS: Basil, parsley, and thyme.

FRUIT: 1 small green apple

NUTS: Pistachios

SERVINGS: 2-3

TIME: 15 MINUTES

DIFFICULTY: EASY

RED POTATO SALAD,
for a PICNIC or ANYTIME

NOTE: This image is from my video. Follow along if you'd like.

Potato Salad reminds me of having a picnic at every meal. It doesn't matter what time of year it is because it's good anytime.

Potato salad can be very particular for a lot of people. From the dressing to what you add in with the potatoes, I think, could probably be up to debate. It's a dish people definitely make their own and that is what I love about potato salad. It's delicious no matter what.

I usually make potato salad with Yukon, white or red potatoes. There may be other varieties but these are my top three. I think they hold up well compared to using Russet potatoes. Again, it's up to you.

As for the dressing, I really like this one because I think it can be used in any potato salad. I do not prefer my potato salad slathered with dressing. I don't think you get to taste all of the other ingredients in the dish when the main ingredient is the dressing.

66 Potato Salad reminds me of having a picnic at every meal.

INGREDIENTS

8–10 Red Potatoes, cut into bite-sized chunks

2 Celery stalks, chopped

4 Cloves Garlic, minced

2–4 Radishes, thinly sliced

2 Green Onions, chopped

Small bunch Parsley, chopped
(save a little for garnish)

1 Tbsp Chives, chopped

DRESSING

½ cup Mayo

⅓ cup Olive Oil

½ tsp dried Dill or 1tsp fresh

1 tsp Garlic Powder

1 ½ Tbsp Stone Ground Mustard or Brown Mustard

1–2 Tbsp Red or White Wine Vinegar

1 tsp Lemon Zest and Juice of ½ Lemon *(optional)*

Dash of Sugar

Salt and Pepper

SERVINGS: 4–6

TIME: 50 MINUTES

DIFFICULTY: EASY

DIRECTIONS

1. In a saucepan, filled with water, add the chopped potatoes and bring the water to a boil. Once the water boils turn down to just a slow rumbling of a boil and cook until the potatoes can easily be pierced with a fork. You don't want the potatoes too soft.

2. While the potatoes are cooking, in a small bowl combine all of the ingredients for the dressing and mix until fully combined. Taste and adjust seasoning, if needed.

3. When the potatoes are finished cooking, drain and let cool before adding the dressing.

4. Add the dressing and gently stir the dressing and the potatoes together.

5. Garnish with some of the parsley and/or chives.

6. Serve at room temperature or place in the refrigerator until ready to serve. Take the salad out of the fridge about 20 minutes before serving.

NOTE: There are a number of other items you can add to potato salad. The possibilities are endless to me. It's really about tradition and what you like. Such as…

- Sweet Pickles
  (then you can omit the sugar in the dressing)
- Hard Boiled Egg
- Sliced Red Onion
- Vinegars—Red, White or Cider
- Paprika
  (a little on top when done mixing in the other ingredients and dressing)
- Bacon, great with white or Yukon potatoes
- Herbs like Basil or Thyme
- Green, Red or Yellow Pepper

ROASTED BEET and ORANGE SALAD with GOAT CHEESE

I was having my two very good friends, Lisa and Debi, over for lunch and I thought this was the perfect salad to make. It's been awhile since I made this. We had a great time together.

Roasting beets is the best way to prepare them, in my opinion. They keep their sweet flavor, they don't taste watered down like boiling them and you don't lose the nutrients. Like anything else, it's best not to over cook them or beets will have a bitter taste to them. I like mixing up the different kinds of beets but feel free to use one type of beets.

I paired the roasted beets with oranges, celery for crunch, goat cheese and toasted walnuts over romaine and arugula lettuce. A perfect easy summer salad to make. The longest time needed was roasting beets.

A nice sliced up baguette bread works well to serve with this salad.

❝ Roasting beets is the best way to prepare them, in my opinion.

INGREDIENTS

3–4 small/medium size Purple Beets, washed, scrubbed, and stems and bottoms cut off

2–3 small Orange Beets, washed, scrubbed, and stems and bottoms cut off

2 stalks Celery with leaves, sliced

1 small Red Onion, thinly sliced

1 large sweet Navel Orange, peeled, separated and sliced or 3 to 4 Clementines peeled and separated

1 small bunch Romaine Lettuce, chopped

A couple handfuls Arugula Lettuce

½ cup Toasted Walnuts

4–6 oz Goat or Feta Cheese

Parsley, chopped for garnish

DRESSING

1 Tbsp Orange Juice

1 Tbsp Orange Zest

1 Tbsp Red Wine Vinegar

2 tsp Balsamic Vinegar

¼ cup Olive Oil

Salt and Pepper

Drizzle of Honey, if desired

SERVINGS: 3

TIME: 1 HOUR

DIFFICULTY: INTERMEDIATE

DIRECTIONS

1. Preheat oven to 400 degrees.

2. Wrap each beet, loosely in foil (not super tight). Place on a parchment lined baking sheet and bake for 1 hour, depending on the size of beets. If small, check at 45 minutes. Beets are done if they can be easily pierced with a fork or knife to the center.

3. Cool slightly and unwrap beets. Skin can easily be rubbed off because the steam from cooking makes it easy to do this. Slice each beet or cut each beet in half, then quartered them and cut them in chunks.

4. Prep oranges. Slice red onion in thin slices. Thinly slice celery and chop up leaf end if desired.

5. Rough chop walnuts. In a sauté pan toast walnuts, on low, until just lightly brown.

6. Chop up romaine lettuce.

7. Slice or spoon goat cheese in small amounts and place in a bowl.

DRESSING

1. In a small mixing bowl, add the olive oil, orange juice, zest, balsamic vinegar and red wine vinegar. Whisk together. Add salt and pepper, taste, adjust salt and pepper and/or honey, if needed. I didn't want the dressing too tart but also not too sweet, for this salad.

PLATING

1. On each plate, place romaine and arugula lettuce and slightly mix together.

2. Place beets and oranges scattered on the plate. No real order is necessary. Then add the onions and scatter the celery on the plate.

3. Add the cheese and walnuts.

4. Garnish with a little chopped parsley.

GREEN BEANS with BACON and SHALLOTS

Green beans are a perfect side dish for any meal. They are delicious, easy and versatile in the many ways you can prepare or add them to your favorite dish.

In this recipe who doesn't like bacon? The shallots and bacon are tasty compliments and flavor for the beans.

Green beans are probably the one and only vegetable Chris likes.

66 Shallots and bacon are tasty compliments for the beans.

INGREDIENTS

1 lb Green Beans, washed, ends trimmed

2 Tbsp Butter

2 Tbsp Olive Oil

Kosher Salt and Pepper

4 slices Bacon, cooked and chopped

1 small Shallot, finely chopped

SERVINGS: 6-8

TIME: 15 MINUTES

DIFFICULTY: EASY

DIRECTIONS

1. In a sauté pan cook bacon until just before bacon is crispy. Cool and chop bacon. Set aside.

2. In a sauté pan heat up butter and oil on low heat.

3. Place beans in a pan and add salt and pepper.

4. Cook until tender. Add in chopped bacon and shallots to beans until heated through.

Notes

LEMON RICE and QUINOA

Rice is a perfect compliment to almost any dish. Pairing rice with quinoa is a great combination. Quinoa is a healthy grain that is full of protein.

A great substitute is using orzo with the rice. You cook it similar to Rice-A-Roni (sautéing the orzo in butter before adding in the rice and broth or water).

Lemon just makes everything taste good with its brightness of flavor.

" Rice is a perfect compliment to most any dish. And, I really like it paired with quinoa.

INGREDIENTS

1 ¼ cup Rice, cooked according to package
(I prefer to use chicken or vegetable broth but water is perfectly fine)

½ cup Quinoa, cooked according to package

Salt

½ medium Sweet Onion, chopped

3-4 Cloves Garlic, minced

1-2 Lemons juiced and zested

Handful Parsley, chopped

2 Tbsp dried Dill, or 4 Tbsp fresh Dill

SERVINGS: 2-3

TIME: 30 MINUTES

DIFFICULTY: INTERMEDIATE

DIRECTIONS

1. Add rice and broth or water to a saucepan and bring to a boil. Add salt. Let it cook for a minute and turn down to a simmer. Cook for about 20 minutes or longer until light and fluffy.

2. Add quinoa and water to a saucepan and bring to a boil. Add salt. Let it cook for a minute and turn down to a simmer. Cook for about 10 minutes or more until light and fluffy.

3. Combine the rice and quinoa together and keep warm.

4. While rice and quinoa is cooking, add onions to a sauté pan on medium-high and cook until translucent.

5. Add in the garlic and cook until aromatic. Add onion mixture to the rice and quinoa and stir.

6. Add in the lemon juice and zest stir until all mixed together.

7. In a small bowl, mix together the dill and parsley and sprinkle over the rice quinoa, add a few slices of lemon on the side.

Notes

MAC and CHEESE

Who doesn't love Mac and Cheese? It's the ultimate of comfort food. The rich creaminess of the cheese, the toasted crunchy topping from the breadcrumbs and the soft chewy like noodles are just deliciousness in your mouth.

I've worked a number of times on making this recipe. I think I got it right with this one. The challenge was to get the amount of cheese and milk portion just right to make that creamy cheesy mac and cheese I knew as a kid, growing up. In fact, this is a remake of my Baked Mac and Cheese in my cookbook that I wrote a number of years ago.

I enjoy this updated version and I hope you do, too. Let's face it, it's all about the cheese in the sauce.

NOTE: It's best to use cheese in a block and grate it yourself instead of using the pre-packaged cheeses. Pre-packaged cheese has a dusting on it and it doesn't melt well for Mac and Cheese.

 Creamy cheese, toasted crunchy toppings, and soft chewy-like noodles are deliciousness in your mouth.

1 lb Large Elbow Macaroni

11 Tbsp Butter

¼ cup Onions, chopped

½ cup Flour

2 cups Milk

2 cups Heavy Whipping Cream

3 ½ cups Cheddar Cheese, grated

1 ½ cups Gruyere Cheese, grated

1 cup Swiss Cheese*, grated

Salt, if needed *(take note that the cheese has a lot of salt in it already)*

1 cup Panko Breadcrumbs

½ tsp White Pepper

¼ tsp Paprika

½ tsp Garlic

2 Tbsp chopped Parsley

If you don't have Swiss cheese, grate 4 cups Cheddar and 2 cups Gruyere.

I think having a two combo grated cheese mixture works best.

SUGGESTED ADDITIONS

Bacon

Chopped Broccoli

Truffle Oil

SERVINGS: 2-3

TIME: 1 HOUR

DIFFICULTY: INTERMEDIATE

DIRECTIONS

1. Preheat oven to 325 degrees and grease the bottom and sides of baking dish.

2. In a sauté pan cook the onions until translucent, when done, place in a small bowl.

3. In a large saucepan, bring water and dash of salt to a boil then add the macaroni. Cook until al dente. Drain and then drizzle a little oil to prevent from sticking together.

4. While the macaroni is cooking, combine the milk and whipping cream together in a bowl.

5. In another bowl combine the grated cheddar, gruyère and swiss cheeses together. Reserve 1 cup for the middle and another cup for the topping.

6. Melt 3 Tbsp of butter in a small bowl and then add 1½ cups of breadcrumbs, salt, white pepper, and garlic.

7. Melt 8 Tbsp of butter in another large saucepan on medium heat. Once the butter has melted slowly add in the flour and whisk together. Keep whisking while cooking the roux for about 2–4 minutes. We're cooking it to get a nice brown color and nutty taste cooking out the flour.

8. Slowly add in milk, continuing to whisk into the roux mixture until well blended. Cook until the sauce thickens.

9. Gradually add in 4 cups of the cheese mixture and stir together until well blended.

10. Add in the cooked macaroni and mix together until blended.

11. Pour half of the macaroni in a baking dish. Sprinkle 1 cup of the cheese over the macaroni. Repeat steps with the rest of the macaroni and remaining cheese.

12. Sprinkle the bread crumb mixture on top.

13. Bake for about 30–35 minutes until thoroughly heated through, the cheese has melted and the bread crumbs are toasted. Cool garnish with chopped parsley, if desired. Serve with your favorite choice of meat and/or salad.

NOTE:

A roux is a flour butter mixture that you cook until bubbly and turns a golden brown. You're basically cooking out the raw flour taste. It is the base for a nice creamy sauce that is key to Macaroni and Cheese. Take your time, it will be worth it.

MUSHROOM and PEA RISOTTO

Risotto reminds me of mac and cheese in a lot of ways. It's another dish that speaks of comfort food.

This recipe takes time and you must pay attention, but it's worth it. Slow cooking is key here and will bring your risotto to perfection.

Cheese is a key ingredient, or you can add in some of your other favorite ingredients — white wine, lemon zest and juice, seafood, herbs, the list goes on. It's worth the time and effort to make risotto.

Give it a try!

66 Risotto is another dish that speaks of comfort food.

INGREDIENTS

5–6 cups Chicken Broth, divided *(may use most or all of broth)*

3 Tbsp Olive Oil, divided

1 ½ lbs Mushrooms, thinly sliced *(I used brown Mushrooms)*

1 cup Peas, frozen

2 Shallots, chopped

1 ½ cups Arborio Rice

½ cup White Wine

Salt and Pepper, to taste

3 Tbsp fresh Parsley

4 Tbsp Butter

⅓ cup Parmesan Cheese, freshly grated

SERVINGS: 4–6

TIME: 40 MINUTES

DIFFICULTY: EASY

DIRECTIONS

1. In a saucepan, warm the broth over low heat.

2. Warm 2 Tbsp olive oil in a large pot over medium high heat. Stir in the mushrooms and cook until soft, about 5 minutes. Remove mushrooms and their liquid and set aside.

3. In a skillet add 1 Tbsp olive oil and stir in the shallots.

4. Cook for about 1 minute. Add rice, stirring to coat with the oil and shallots and continue to cook about 2 minutes until the rice becomes a pale golden color. Add in the wine and stir constantly until the wine is absorbed.

5. Add ½ cup of broth to the rice and stir until the broth is absorbed. Continue adding ½ cup of broth at a time, stirring continuously until the liquid is absorbed and the rice is al dente, about 30 minutes.

6. Remove from heat and stir in mushrooms with the liquid, peas, butter, and Parmesan cheese until mixed in with the rice.

7. Season with salt, pepper and parsley.

Notes

PEAS PESTO with SUN-DRIED TOMATOES

This is one of my favorite appetizers to make.

The sweetness of the mashed peas with the tart and tangy sun dried tomatoes make for a perfect pair. Salty grated Parmesan cheese and finely chopped parsley or basil compliments it nicely.

If you are looking for a perfect appetizer to bring to a party or serve as the host, this is it.

 NOTE: This image is from my video. Follow along if you'd like.

" The sweetness of mashed peas with tart and tangy sun dried tomatoes make for a perfect pair.

INGREDIENTS

1 Pkg frozen Peas, thawed
(you can use fresh as well)

½ cup grated Parmesan
Cheese

1 cup Basil

½ cup Parsley

2–3 Cloves Garlic

1 small Lemon Zest

2 Tbsp Lemon Juice

Salt and Pepper

¼ cup or more Olive Oil

¼ cup Sun-dried Tomatoes

1 Baguette
(or crackers or veggies for dipping)

SERVINGS: 4–6

TIME: 10 MINUTES

DIFFICULTY: EASY

DIRECTIONS

1. Thaw the frozen peas by running under warm water *(I prefer this over microwave)* and pat dry.

2. Chop up the sun-dried tomatoes.

3. In a food processor add in the peas, grated Parmesan cheese, basil, parsley, garlic, lemon zest and juice, and salt and pepper. Pulse several times to blend it all together.

4. Slowly add in the olive oil until you get a good consistency.

5. Taste and if needed add a little more salt, lemon juice or olive oil.

6. Slice the baguette, diagonally, in thick slices, about ¼–½ inches.

7. Brush each slice with olive oil. Toast in the oven for a few minutes, until the edges are just turning golden brown.

8. Turn the slices over and toast the other side.

9. Spread a little of the pea pesto on each baguette slice. Top with the chopped sun-dried tomatoes and a pinch of grated Parmesan cheese.

Notes

SPAGHETTI SQUASH WITH ROASTED TOMATOES

Spaghetti squash when cooked spooned out looks like spaghetti noodles.

Spaghetti squash is a versatile vegetable and compliments most anything you may add to it. For this simple dish I wanted to create something that would go with most any protein or just by itself.

Roasted tomatoes add a little sweet and tangy flavor to the mellow squash. Sprinkled with a little cheese and chopped parsley makes it a perfect side dish. Feel free to add your favorite vegetables such as mushrooms and onion.

Treat spaghetti squash like spaghetti pasta. It's great with a meat sauce as well.

 Roasted tomatoes add a little sweet and tangy flavor to the mellow squash.

INGREDIENTS

1 large Spaghetti Squash

Olive Oil

2 cups Cherry Tomatoes

2 Garlic Cloves, chopped

2 tsp Thyme

Salt and Pepper

A handful Parsley, chopped

Parmesan Cheese, grated

SERVINGS: 3-4

TIME: 1 HOUR

DIFFICULTY: INTERMEDIATE

DIRECTIONS

1. Preheat oven to 375 degrees.

2. Cut spaghetti squash length wise in half and scoop out seed pulp. Drizzle with olive oil and sprinkle salt and pepper on squash. Roast squash for about 50 minutes until tender and able to scoop out with a fork.

3. Once squash is done cooking let it rest and cool down for about 15 minutes.

4. In the meantime place tomatoes in a shallow baking pan and drizzle with olive oil and sprinkle with salt and pepper. Roast for about 20–30 minutes, just before they pop and split open.

5. Scoop out spaghetti squash pulp (it really does look like spaghetti, I love it) and place in a baking dish.

6. Mix in the roasted tomatoes, thyme, salt and pepper to taste and put in the oven to heat up.

7. Garnish with parsley and grated cheese!

Notes

STUFFED MINI PEPPERS
with CHEESE and BACON

Mini peppers are a very versatile vegetable. They are colorful, have a hint of sweetness, and are perfect for appetizers.

This is another of my favorite appetizers to make. When the peppers are filled with the creamy cheese, salty bacon and herbs you have a perfect bite.

These mini peppers are a crowd pleaser for any occasion.

 The creaminess of cheese, salty bacon and herbs creates a perfect bite.

INGREDIENTS

12 or more Mini Bell Peppers, sliced in half

1 cup Ricotta Cheese

½ cup grated Parmesan Cheese

Salt and Pepper to taste

3-4 slices Bacon, chopped

1 small bunch Parsley, chopped

½ tsp Garlic Powder

1-2 Green Onions, chopped

Red Pepper Flakes
(optional)

DIRECTIONS

1. Preheat oven to 425 degrees.
2. Line a baking sheet with parchment paper.
3. Slice each mini pepper in half and place on baking sheet.
4. Cook bacon until done, but not overly crispy, drain, pat dry, and chop.
5. In a bowl combine the ricotta cheese, Parmesan cheese, chopped bacon, parsley, garlic powder, chopped green onions and a few of the red pepper flakes.
6. Add Salt and Pepper to taste.
7. Place about 1 heaping teaspoon of the cheese mixture on each mini Red Pepper.
8. Bake for about 5-10 minutes until the cheese mixture has melted and is slightly brown on top and the mini peppers are tender but not soft. Best if served warm.

SERVINGS: 4-6

TIME: 1/2 HOUR

DIFFICULTY: INTERMEDIATE

Notes

TWICE BAKED POTATOES

Who doesn't like potatoes? There are so many different ways to prepare them and one of them I really like is twice baked potatoes. Since it's been a while since I've made them I thought now was a good time. Whew. Glad I did because I forgot how amazingly tasty they are.

I can think of many ways to make twice baked potatoes. The possibilities are left to your imagination.

 NOTE: This image is from my video. Follow along if you'd like.

> " There are so many different ways to prepare potatoes and one of them I really like is twice baked.

INGREDIENTS

3 med–large Potatoes
(Russet work best for this)

2–4 Tbsp Butter

Salt and Pepper

4–6 Bacon strips, chopped

2 Green Onions, finely chopped

1 cup + Cheddar Cheese, grated *(save some for topping)*

¼ cup or more Sour Cream

Salt and Pepper

Optional: Cream, if needed

GARNISH

Sour Cream

Chives

Cheddar Cheese, grated

SERVINGS: 2

TIME: 1 HOUR 45 MINUTES

DIFFICULTY: INTERMEDIATE

DIRECTIONS

1. Preheat oven to 400 degrees.

2. Line a baking sheet with parchment paper. Place the potatoes on the baking sheet. *If you don't want a crunchy skin then I would rub the potatoes with a little canola or olive oil.* Bake for about 1 hour, depending on how large the potatoes are. The potatoes are done when they feel soft or if a strong toothpick easily goes through.

3. While the potatoes are baking, heat up a sauté pan and cook the bacon on medium heat to desired doneness. When done, chop up the bacon. *Many people have strong opinions about how they like their bacon—I prefer mine a little crispy.*

4. While the potatoes are cooling down, chop up the green onions and grate the cheese. Turn down the heat to 350 degrees.

5. In a bowl, add the butter, bacon and 1 cup of cheddar and sour cream.

6. With a sharp knife cut each potato in half. Gently scoop out the inside into the mixing bowl. *Don't go right down to the skin because you want to leave just enough to give the potato some support to hold the inside mixture.*

7. Mash the inside of the potatoes and mix into the butter, bacon, sour cream and cheese. Season the mixture with salt and pepper and green onions. Mix well.

8. Add the potato mixture into the potato shells. It's ok to fill the shells a little over the top into a lovely mound.

9. Top the potatoes with the reminder of the shredded cheese and bake for about another 15–25 minutes until piping hot.

10. Serve with sour cream and chives.

NOTE: When making regular baked potatoes I generally put them on the oven rack and poke them about two times with a fork to let out steam. For twice baked potatoes, I think it's best to rub them with a little oil. This still gives the slightly crispy skin that I like.

Baked
Goods

BLUEBERRY PANCAKES

Making pancakes always reminds me of my brother, Roger. When he got older he was kind of like the king of pancake making. On the weekends he would always make the family pancakes. So every time I make pancakes for my kids or anybody else, it always reminds me of my brother. He does it for his kids and everyone. He is the king of making pancakes, so I hope I do him proud.

I enjoy making these blueberry pancakes for brunch.

 My brother, Roger, was the king of pancake making growing up.

INGREDIENTS

¾ cup Milk

1 ½ Tbsp Lemon Juice

1 cup Flour

1 Tbsp Sugar

1 Tbsp Baking Powder

½ tsp Baking Soda

½ tsp Salt

1 Egg

2 Tbsp melted Butter

1 cup fresh Blueberries

Butter for griddle

SERVINGS: 2

TIME: 25 MINUTES

DIFFICULTY: EASY

DIRECTIONS

1. Mix the milk with the lemon juice and let it rest for a few minutes. *You could just use buttermilk here but I like the hint of lemon juice in the pancake batter. I basically make my own buttermilk.*

2. Whisk the dry ingredients together in a bowl.

3. In another bowl, whisk together the egg, milk and melted butter.

4. Stir the wet ingredients into the dry ingredients until just combined. *Remember that you don't want to over mix the batter. The pancakes had a good chance of being more flat instead of fluffy.*

5. Gently fold in the blueberries.

6. Heat your griddle or pan over medium heat. Melt a little butter in the pan, this will give the pancakes that brown crispy outside *(don't over cook, it can happen fast).*

7. Pour the batter onto the griddle. Cook each pancake, for about 1–2 minutes on each side, until you see tiny little bubbles around the edges and top, and lightly brown on the bottom. Flip and cook the other side for about another 1–2 minutes until crispy on the outside and tender inside.

8. Serve with butter and warm maple syrup or other topping, you desire.

Notes

CORN BEEF HASH & EGGS

I really like Corn Beef. It's rich, seasoned, and versatile in a lot of dishes.

This past year I made Corn Beef sandwiches for me and Chris. I didn't make the traditional Corn Beef and Cabbage with Potatoes (which is still a favorite of mine), instead, I added sauerkraut and a homemade thousand island dressing. After making several sandwiches I thought about making a hash.

This is a wonderful breakfast, brunch, or anytime of day dish. The meat is already seasoned, so it is a matter of what you want to add to make the hash.

Hash is a great way to use leftover meat by adding in potatoes, onions, and fresh flavors.

 Corn Beef is rich and seasoned and so versatile in a lot of dishes.

INGREDIENTS

Leftover Corn Beef, shredded or chopped in bite-size pieces *(use as much as you prefer, depending on ratio of meat and vegetables you want to serve)*

Salt and Pepper

Olive Oil

1 small Onion, chopped

3–4 White or Yukon Gold Potatoes, chopped into bite size pieces

1 large Carrot, chopped

1–2 Cloves Garlic, minced

½ Green Pepper, chopped

½ Red Pepper, chopped

1 tsp Thyme

GARNISHES

1 Green Onion, chopped

Small bunch Parsley, chopped

Mild or Medium Cheddar Cheese, grated *(optional)*

Fried Eggs *(optional)*

SERVINGS: 2

TIME: 45 MINUTES

DIFFICULTY: INTERMEDIATE

DIRECTIONS

1. Prep and chop your vegetables and meat.

2. In a heavy sauté pan or cast iron skillet, heat butter and olive oil. Add in the potatoes and cook on medium to high heat. Season with salt and pepper and cook until brown. Remove potatoes to a bowl.

3. In the same pan add a little more butter and olive oil and heat. Add in the onions, carrots, peppers, and season with salt and pepper. Cook until just soft.

4. Add in the garlic until aromatic.

5. Add in thyme. Continue to cook for another 5 minutes.

6. Add in the potatoes and corn beef and stir all of the ingredients together. Continue cooking until heated through, about another 10–15 minutes.

7. While the corn beef hash is cooking on low, in another pan, fry your eggs, as you desire.

8. Garnish with green onions, parsley and cheddar cheese, if desired, and serve.

Notes

HASH BROWNS EGG CASSEROLE

This casserole is a great breakfast or brunch recipe to feed a few or all your family and friends.

With a little prep, you can make it the night before and be ready to bake it in the morning. Just take it out of the refrigerator and rest for about 30 minutes before baking. You can enjoy a hot breakfast and relax with family and friends the rest of the morning. This is hearty, scrumptious and full of good things to wake up to in the morning.

A benefit of this dish is you can completely make it your own by adding in whatever meat, veggies and cheese you want. No matter how many times you make it you'll always find another way to make it new again. I love a recipe that has so much variety and versatility in what you can put in it.

66 This is hearty, scrumptious and full of good things to wake up to in the morning.

INGREDIENTS

1–2 Tbsp Butter or Olive Oil

½ lb Sausage *(I used Mild Italian)*

1 small or ½ large Red Pepper, diced

⅓ cup Onion, diced

⅓ cup Parsley, chopped

1 tsp Hot Paprika

1 large Clove Garlic, minced

Salt and Pepper

4–6 small White or Yukon Potatoes, grated or
1 lb frozen Hash Browns
(I used grated potatoes)

5–6 large Eggs

⅓ cup Cream

½ cup Milk

1 cup Cheese
(I used Sharp Cheddar Cheese, save a little for topping)

Chives, for garnish

SERVINGS: 2–3

TIME: 1 HOUR 30 MINUTES

DIFFICULTY: INTERMEDIATE

DIRECTIONS

1. Preheat oven to 375 degrees. Grease baking dish.
   I used a medium baking dish.

2. Heat butter in a sauté pan. Cook onions and pepper with a little salt and pepper until vegetables are tender. Add in garlic and stir for about 1 minute. Remove and place vegetables in a bowl.

3. *Optional:* Heat sauté pan and lightly brown hash browns on one side and then fold over and brown the other. Add Salt and Pepper. Remove from the pan.

4. In a sauté pan, cook the sausage until done.

5. In a baking dish, layer the potatoes first, sprinkle a little cheese and add in sausage and vegetables.

6. In a bowl, add eggs, cream, milk, and salt and pepper. Whisk together. Pour over the potato sausage vegetable mixture.

7. Bake for about 40–45 minutes until lightly brown on top and the knife comes out clean when inserted. Don't over bake or it may come out a little dry.

8. *Optional:* Just before finishing baking, add a little more cheese on top and bake until melted.

9. Top with chives. Serve and Enjoy.

INGREDIENT SUGGESTIONS

- **Meats:** Sausage, ham, bacon, turkey sausage or bacon.
- **Vegetables:** Red, green and/or yellow peppers, onion, mushrooms, spinach, wilted kale, green onions, zucchini, butternut squash.
- **Cheeses:** Cheddar cheese *(mild, medium, sharp)*, provolone, feta, mozzarella, pepper jack *(for a little spice)*.
- **Herbs and Spices:** Italian seasoning, thyme, chives, parsley, paprika *(hot or smoked)*, garlic, nutmeg, red pepper flakes.

POTATO PANCAKES

These Potato Pancakes pair well with my Brisket and Green Beans.

They are a quick and easy side to make and compliment many dishes. You can even eat them on their own as a snack.

66 These easy-to-make potato pancakes are a crowd favorite and go great with EVERYTHING!

INGREDIENTS

6 medium Russet Potatoes

1 medium Onion

Kosher Salt and Ground Black Pepper

2 Egg Whites, beaten together

¼ cup Chives or Parsley, finely chopped

Canola Oil, for frying

SERVINGS: 8-10

TIME: 30 MINUTES

DIFFICULTY: EASY

DIRECTIONS

1. Wash and peel potatoes.

2. Use a box grater or food processor to grate potatoes.

3. Place grated potatoes in a bowl with cold water and about ½ tsp lemon juice *(to prevent browning until ready to prepare into pancakes)*.

4. Grate or finely chop the onion.

5. Drain potatoes and onion in a strainer, lined with a cheesecloth, and squeeze as much water as you can from the potatoes and onion.

6. In a bowl combine the potatoes, onion, egg whites, salt, pepper and chives or parsley and mix all together.

7. Heat oil in a non-stick sauté pan. Use about 1-2 large tablespoons of potato mixture, drop into the pan and flatten with a spatula. Cook for about 3 minutes, until brown.

8. Using a spatula and spoon gently flip over to cook the other side. Place on a plate lined with a paper towel to soak up left over oil.

9. Lightly salt while still hot or grate some Parmesan cheese on potatoes. Keep warm.

10. Add more oil when necessary and cook pancakes in batches until all the potato mixture is used up.

Notes

BANANA CHOCOLATE 'CHIP' MUFFINS

I think the combo of banana and chocolate were made for each other. These are just absolute deliciousness.

Ripe bananas are best to use because they have so much flavor and sweetness.

When I can, I use the combination of brown sugar and white sugar when it doesn't affect the end results, but enhances it in a different way. Why may you ask? I like the kind of rustic sweetness and moistness brown sugar gives. I use oil with butter in this recipe. Butter will give that extra boost of flavor and oil will give moistness. The sour cream will balance out the sweet taste with a little tang and richness.

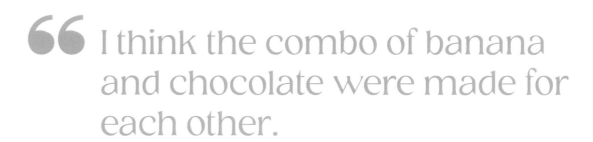

" I think the combo of banana and chocolate were made for each other.

INGREDIENTS

3-4 ripe Bananas, mashed

1 tsp Vanilla

2 Eggs, room temperature

¾ cup Canola or Vegetable Oil

¼ cup Butter, melted

1 ¼ cup Sugar

½ cup Sour Cream

3 cups Flour

1 tsp Baking Powder

½ tsp Baking Soda

½ tsp Salt

2-4 oz Chocolate, chopped

Walnuts, chopped (optional)

DIRECTIONS

1. Preheat oven to 350 degrees.

2. In a bowl combine the flour, baking powder, baking soda and salt.

3. With a mixer, cream the butter. Add in the sugars and mix until thoroughly combined.

4. Add in the oil, vanilla and bananas and mix.

5. Beat in eggs, one at a time.

6. Slowly add the flour into the wet ingredients and mix until just combined. Don't over mix the batter.

7. Fold in the chocolate and nuts (optional).

8. Line muffin tin with paper cups.

9. Spoon batter into muffin tin.

10. Bake muffins for 15-18 minutes.

SERVINGS: 4-6

TIME: 1 HOUR

DIFFICULTY: INTERMEDIATE

Notes

CINNAMON ROLLS

My daughter has the patience and is so much better than I when it comes to baking with yeast. She is my baker. It is challenging to wait for the yeast to foam and the dough to rise twice.

I love making these because it teaches me patience, which you need when baking. Patience pays off when these lovely, soft, and delicious cinnamon rolls come out of the oven.

I've made these rolls several times and this recipe is a success! It helps if you can snuggly roll the dough into a log. With my small hands I haven't been able to roll it as snug as I would like, but these cinnamon rolls still turn out delicious.

I think this will be my go to for Sunday mornings, or anytime I feel like having something that is filled with the warm spice of cinnamon.

 My go-to for Sunday mornings or any time I feel like having something filled with the warm spice of cinnamon.

INGREDIENTS

1 cup Milk, warm

1 packet Quick Active Dry Yeast

⅓ cup Sugar + 1 Tbsp

1 tsp Salt

¼ cup Buttermilk

1 Egg

6 Tbsp Butter, melted

4 ½–5 cups Flour
(start with 4 cups and add as needed for a tacky, not sticky dough)

FILLING

½ cup Butter, softened

1 cup packed Brown Sugar

3 Tbsp Cinnamon
(I like cinnamon so I added 2 Tbs more)

¼ tsp Nutmeg, grated

1 tsp Cornstarch

¼ cup Walnuts, finely chopped
(optional)

1 Egg, beaten *(for egg wash)*

ICING

2 oz Cream Cheese, room temperature

2 Tbsp Butter, softened

1 tsp Vanilla

1 tsp fresh Lemon Juice and Zest *(or Orange Juice and Zest)*

1 ¼ cup Powdered Sugar
(more or less depending on the consistency you want.)

SERVINGS: 6-7

TIME: 2 HOURS 30 MINUTES

DIFFICULTY: INTERMEDIATE

DIRECTIONS

1. Preheat oven to 350 degrees.

2. In a measuring cup, warm up the milk to 110 degrees. It will feel like warm bath water.

3. Stir in 1 Tbsp sugar, then add the yeast. Gently stir the yeast and let it stand until you see the yeast foam up, about 5–10 minutes.

4. In a small bowl whisk together buttermilk, butter and egg until the egg is mixed in.

5. In another bowl whisk together 2 cups of flour and salt. Reserve the other 2 ½–3 cups of flour in a separate bowl.

6. In a mixer bowl, fitted with a dough hook, add the yeast mixture and remaining sugar. Stir on low for about 2 minutes.

7. Pour buttermilk mixture into yeast mixture and stir for about 1–2 minutes more.

8. Pour 2 cups of the flour and salt into the mixer and stir on low until incorporated.

9. Add about ¼ cup of flour at a time and continue adding ¼ cup at a time until the dough cleans the sides and the bottom of the bowl and is no longer sticky, but tacky to the touch. Don't worry if you don't use all of the flour.

10. The dough is ready to knead. Remove the dough and on a clean counter or cutting board, dusted with flour, knead for about 5–10 minutes.

11. Grease a large bowl and place dough in the bowl. Cover with plastic wrap and a warm dish towel. Place dough in a warm room temperature area and let the dough rise until it doubles in size. It may take about 1–1½ hours.

Continued...

FILLING and CUTTING ROLLS

1. In a medium size bowl, stir together brown sugar, cinnamon, nutmeg, cornstarch and walnuts *(optional)*.

2. After the dough has risen, lightly punch it down and let it rest for about 2–3 minutes. Flour a large clean surface and then roll out dough into a large rectangle shape, about 12 inches x 20 inches.

3. Spread the butter over the dough, making sure to leave about ½ inch dough untouched on one of the longer end sides. Sprinkle brown sugar mixture evenly all over the buttered dough, making sure filling doesn't fall off the sides. Lightly press the sugar mixture into the butter.

4. Brush the end of the untouched dough with the egg wash.

5. Starting from the longer end, roll the dough up as snug as you can into a log shape roll. Finish with the plain side of the dough and seal the dough together, pinching to seal if needed. Cut off the uneven ends to square it off.

6. Grease pans and line with parchment paper. You can use two smaller pans, a 9x13 pan, large cake pan or whatever pan you have to fit the rolls in.

7. Cut dough into 2 inch slices and place in pans, allowing enough space for the rolls to expand and get puffy. You don't want them to touch before rising again. Cover pans lightly with plastic wrap and a warm dish towel.

8. Let the rolls rise, for about 1–1½ hours or until they have risen and are touching the sides.

9. Bake rolls in a preheated 350 oven for about 15–18 minutes until they turn slightly golden brown. Try not to over bake them.

ICING

1. While the rolls are cooling, in a bowl mix together cream cheese and butter with a hand mixer.

2. Stir in vanilla, lemon juice and zest and blend together.

3. Add powdered sugar and slowly mix together until fully incorporated, smooth and the desired consistency.

4. Spread icing on rolls. If still a little warm, let the icing melt into the rolls. Wait a few minutes for rolls to cool before icing them.

Practice and patience pays off for lovely, soft, delicious Cinnamon Rolls.

Notes

CINNAMON WALNUT ROLL UPS

I remember making baklava for the holidays growing up and have made it a number of times over the years. Ground up walnuts, plenty of cinnamon rolled up into a flaky phyllo dough and drizzle with honey and brown sugar syrup. It's a delicious little crunch of a treat for any time.

Recently, I was making my White Chicken Bean Chili and I felt like something with cinnamon would go well with it. Baklava came to mind, but didn't have that kind of time. I wondered if rolling up the dough with the mixture instead of the layers and layers it takes to make baklava would work. It did!

The hardest part of this recipe is being careful with the phyllo dough because it's a little delicate. Enjoy this easier version of a delicious sweet treat.

 If you like Baklava I think you'll like this. It's very similar, yet one difference, it's easier to make.

INGREDIENTS

2 ¼ cup Walnuts, ground up
(tip: toast the walnuts before grinding)

¼ cup Sugar

2 Tbsp Cinnamon

12 sheets Phyllo Dough,
thawed at room temperature

½ cup Unsalted Butter, melted

¼ tsp Salt

SYRUP

½ cup Honey

⅓ cup Sugar

¼ cup Brown Sugar

¼ tsp Salt

⅓ cup Water

2 tsp Lemon Juice

SERVINGS: 4-6

TIME: 1 HOUR

DIFFICULTY: INTERMEDIATE

DIRECTIONS

1. Preheat oven to 350 degrees.

2. In a bowl add the walnuts, sugar and cinnamon and salt and stir until well combined.

3. On a large piece of parchment paper place a sheet of phyllo dough and brush with butter, lay another sheet on top and brush with butter and lay a third sheet of phyllo dough on top and brush with butter. *Place a damp cloth on top of the remaining phyllo dough to prevent drying out.*

4. Use ⅓ cup of the walnut mixture and evenly sprinkle it all around on top of the three layers of phyllo dough. Use your spoon or fingers to evenly spread it around, if needed.

5. On the long side of the phyllo dough, roll it up jelly-roll style as snug as possible. Cut rolled up phyllo dough in half or if you'd like, cut it up into thirds. Repeat with the other sheets of phyllo dough.

6. On a baking sheet lined with parchment paper, bake the cinnamon walnut roll ups for about 12-15 minutes until lightly brown. Let cool.

7. While the rollups are baking, in a small saucepan add the honey, sugars, salt, water and lemon juice. Bring it to a small boil, turn down the heat and let it simmer for about 10 minutes. Take off heat and let it cool for about another 15 minutes.

8. Drizzle the cinnamon walnut roll ups with the honey syrup and sprinkle the remaining walnut mixture on top. Gently press walnuts down on the rolls. Let it set for about 10 minutes before serving.

Notes

PUMPKIN BREAD with STREUSEL TOPPING

Is there anyone who doesn't like pumpkin? Ok, a few, I know. Since I lived on a farm for many years and we grew pumpkins, I had to create a recipe for pumpkin bread, and this is one of my favorite loaf breads to make.

I liked pumpkin bread as a kid and love it as an adult, so do my kids. There is something about pumpkin, *(another very versatile vegetable to make sweet or savory)*, that makes a delicious bread. Pumpkin bread is perfect in the morning, afternoon snack or dessert.

The warm spices of the Pumpkin Bread and a cup of coffee or tea is a perfect combination to appreciate the moment and beauty of a crisp fall day.

NOTE: This image is from my video. Follow along if you'd like.

66 On those crisp fall days you can't go wrong with the warm spices and moist bread.

INGREDIENTS

3 cups Flour

1 ½ tsp Baking Soda

1 tsp Baking Powder

½ tsp Salt

2 tsp Pumpkin Spice

2 tsp Cinnamon

1 tsp Ginger

½ tsp Nutmeg

¾ cup Unsalted Butter, room temperature

2 cups Sugar (or 1½ cups White Sugar and ½ cup Brown Sugar)

3 Eggs, room temperature

½ cup Sour Cream or Greek Yogurt

1 14.5 oz can Pumpkin Puree

1 tsp Vanilla

½ cup Walnuts or Pecans, chopped (optional)

STREUSEL TOPPING

4 Tbsp Butter, room temperature

½ cup Flour

¼ tsp Salt

⅓ cup Brown Sugar

1 tsp Cinnamon

½ tsp Ginger

¼ tsp Nutmeg

1 Tbsp Flax Seed (optional)

SERVINGS: 8-10

TIME: 55 MINUTES

DIFFICULTY: EASY

DIRECTIONS

1. Preheat oven to 350 degrees.

2. In a large bowl combine the flour, baking soda, baking powder and salt and stir together.

3. Add the pumpkin pie spice, cinnamon, ginger and nutmeg to the flour mixture and stir thoroughly until combined.

4. In a mixer bowl, cream the butter. Add in the sugar and cream until thoroughly mixed together.

5. Add in the eggs, one at a time, beating until combined after each egg. Mix until creamy and fluffy.

6. Add in the sour cream, vanilla and pumpkin puree, mix together.

7. Gradually add in the flour mixture, a little at a time, until just combined.

8. Pour the batter into a greased flour bread pan. Gently fold in the nuts (optional).

STREUSEL

1. In a small bowl mix together the flour, salt, brown sugar, cinnamon, ginger, nutmeg and flax seeds.

2. Add in the butter and stir until completely combined and the mixture is crumbly looking.

3. Spoon the mixture on top of the pumpkin bread and gently press down.

4. Bake for about 65–70 minutes until a toothpick or knife inserted in the center comes out clean or just a little crumbly.

5. Let cool completely before removing from the pan and serving.

Notes

PIZZA DOUGH for EVERY KIND of PIZZA

I don't think I know of a person that doesn't like pizza. Usually the big questions are all about thin or regular crust and what kind of toppings to put on the pizza. There is so much variety you can create with toppings.

For me, it depends on my mood. First, I decide on the sauce—red or white. Then the toppings, and that depends on what I have in the fridge, or have pre-bought the toppings.

This time around, I had a great time being in the kitchen making pizzas with my daughter, Molly, and daughter-in-law, Isabel. We made three different pizzas with different sauces and toppings. It was a good time and I loved tasting our different kinds of pizza. They were all so delicious to eat.

So let's make pizza!

 The big questions are all about thin or regular crust and what kind of toppings to put on the pizza.

INGREDIENTS

1 cup warm Water
(105–110 degrees)

1 Tbsp Sugar

2 ¼ tsp or 1 packet Quick
Active Dry Yeast

1 Tbsp Olive Oil

2–2 ½ cups Flour

1 tsp Salt

RED SAUCE

1 15 oz can Tomato Sauce

1 6 oz can Tomato Paste

1 Tbsp Olive Oil

½ tsp Salt

1 Tbsp Garlic Powder

1 tsp Onion Powder

2 tsp Italian Seasonings

½ tsp Oregano

Pinch or more of Sugar, if
needed

*This makes a thicker sauce then using
a 28oz can crushed tomatoes and
tomato paste. I use an immersion
blender to make the sauce smooth if
using crushed tomatoes.*

WHITE SAUCE

1 Tbsp Butter

1 Tbsp Flour

⅔ cup Milk

Dash of Salt and Pepper

1 tsp Garlic, minced or
½ tsp Garlic Powder

2 Tbsp grated Parmesan
Cheese

*This makes about 1 or 2 pizzas. If
you double the recipe you can make
enough sauce for about 4 small pizzas.*

DIRECTIONS

1. Preheat oven 450 degrees.

2. Add warm water, 105–110 degrees, in a large bowl. Add in the yeast and sugar, stir to combine and then let sit for about 5 minutes until it foams up or is frothy.

3. Add in the olive oil, then flour, and salt and mix until the flour mixture forms a ball. The dough will be a little sticky. Mix by hand or with a mixer using the bread hook.

4. Transfer dough to a bowl greased with oil and turn the dough so all of it is lightly greased with oil.

5. I recommend letting the dough rest for about 30–45 minutes to rise, but it's not necessary, before transferring the dough to a floured surface and knead until smooth.

6. If using a pizza stone, *(from what you may have seen in my video making pizza dough with my daughter and daughter-in-law)*, I recommend heating up the pizza stone before placing the dough on it. It'll help in evenly baking through the center of the dough.

7. When working with the pizza dough, be patient, it may take a little time. Use your hands or a rolling pin to gently push, roll and/or stretch the dough into the shape you want. It may spring back a little. Keep at it until you get the desired thickness and shape.

8. Par-bake and prick your pizza dough before adding the sauce and toppings. This will help in having the dough cook all the way through, not be soft or soggy in the middle, and prevent air bubbles forming in the dough. If wanting a crispier crust on the bottom sprinkle some corn meal on the bottom of the pizza stone/pan before baking.

9. Let cool before adding the sauce, cheese and toppings.

Continued...

RED SAUCE

1. In a saucepan add the tomato paste and olive oil and cook for about 1–2 minutes on medium heat.

2. Add in the garlic and onion powder, Italian seasonings, oregano, salt and sugar. Stir and cook for about another minute.

3. Add in the tomato sauce and cook for about 2–3 minutes until heated through and the sauce has thickened.

4. Cool before spreading the sauce on the pizza dough.

WHITE SAUCE

1. In a small saucepan, melt the butter and then whisk in the flour. Continue to whisk for about a minute or more to cook the flour. But don't let the flour brown.

2. Slowly add in the milk whisking constantly until smooth. Add in the Parmesan cheese and continue to cook the sauce until it is bubbly and has thickened.

3. Cool before adding to the pizza.

ASSEMBLE AND BAKE

1. Add the sauce, vegetables, ⅓ of the grated cheese, meats and then the remaining cheese. If not using vegetables add the cheese and then the meat.

2. Bake pizza for about 12–15 minutes until the cheese has melted and the crust and cheese has turned golden brown.

3. Cool slightly before cutting the pizza pie. Time for Pizza!

TOPPING SUGGESTIONS

Meat:
Pepperoni
Salami
Chicken
Sausage
Canadian Bacon
Bacon

Veggies:
Onion
Red Onion
Green Onion
Spinach
Mushroom
Olives
Green Peppers
Sun-dried Tomatoes

Cheese:
Mozzarella
Provolone
Parmesan
Asiago

I go from a Margherita pizza, to three kinds of meat with onions, mushrooms, olives, green peppers, to chicken, red or green onions, mushrooms, spinach and sun-dried tomatoes and of course cheese.

SERVINGS: 4–6

TIME: 1 HOUR

DIFFICULTY: INTERMEDIATE

Notes

NOTE
If I'm adding more than a couple of vegetables, I'll add the vegetables first, then about 1/3 of the cheese, then meat and then the rest of the cheese. I think this helps the vegetables from over cooking or browning before the pizza is fully baked.

APPLE CAKE, A LITTLE FANCY

Sometimes you need a cake that is simply delicious and easy to make. This Apple Cake is a fancy, delicate cake with just enough sweetness.

The cake has a light fluffy texture, a subtle tartness from the apples and is finished with powdered sugar. It can also be versatile by changing out the apples for another fruit.

Enjoy it anytime of day whether alongside a cup of coffee, a get together with friends, or a dessert for a special dinner.

 Sometimes you need a cake that is just simply delicious. This is it.

INGREDIENTS

1 cup All Purpose Flour

1 tsp Baking Powder

¼ tsp Salt

½ cup Unsalted Butter, melted

⅔ cup Sugar + 1 Tbsp
(to sprinkle on top before baking)

2 large Eggs, room
temperature

1 tsp Vanilla

2 large Apples, peeled and
cut into small chunks
*(Braeburn, Granny Smith, Gala, or
other)*

1 Tbsp Lemon Juice,
with ½ tsp Lemon Zest

Powdered Sugar for dusting
(optional)

SERVINGS: 4-6

TIME: 1 HOUR 30 MINUTES

DIFFICULTY: INTERMEDIATE

DIRECTIONS

1. Preheat oven to 375 degrees. Prepare a 9 inch cake pan. Cut a circle of parchment paper to fit the bottom of the cake pan and grease sides and bottom of paper. Or use a 9 inch springform pan and grease as well.

2. In a small bowl, whisk together flour, baking powder and salt.

3. In a small bowl combine the apples and lemon juice and set aside.

4. In a large bowl, combine sugar, eggs and vanilla. With a hand mixer mix until fully combined.

5. Mix ½ of the flour into the egg mixture, followed by half the melted butter. Repeat with the rest of the flour followed by the butter until all ingredients have been incorporated.

6. Add apples and fold into the batter. Pour the batter into the prepared pan and smooth into an even layer.

7. Gently tap the cake pan to pop any air bubbles.

8. Bake for about 40-45 minutes or until a knife or toothpick inserted in the center comes out clean.

9. Cool pan on a rack for about 15-20 minutes. Gently run a knife around the edge to loosen the cake from the pan. Carefully, with a plate over the cake, gently turn cake over onto a plate or release cake from the spring form and cool completely.

10. Dust cake with powdered sugar.

Notes

APPLE CINNAMON STREUSEL COFFEE CAKE with MAPLE SYRUP GLAZE

I don't know about you, but I love the warm spices of cinnamon and nutmeg, and the sweet tart taste of apples, all year long.

This cake is a favorite during the Fall season. Warm spices, apple or pumpkin butter, apple cider and sour cream create a flavorful cake.

This coffee cake is a different version of my Spice Bundt Cake. I like it when you can change up a recipe and create another scrumptious, tasty baked goodness.

Enjoy!

NOTE: This image is from my video. Follow along if you'd like.

 This coffee cake isn't just for breakfast with a cup of coffee but for anytime of the day.

INGREDIENTS

2 cups All Purpose Flour

8 Tbsp Butter, room temperature

2 Tbsp Baking Powder

¼ tsp Baking Soda

2 Tbsp Cinnamon

¼ tsp Nutmeg

½ tsp Salt

1 cup Brown Sugar

2 tsp Vanilla

2 large Eggs, room temperature

⅓ cup Apple Cider

2 Tbsp Maple Syrup

⅔ cup Sour Cream

½ cup Pumpkin or Apple Butter

STREUSEL

1 cup Brown Sugar

1 ½ Tbsp Cinnamon

¾ cup Flour

6-8 Tbsp Butter

Dash of Salt

1 cup Apples, diced *(1-2 apples)*

½ cup sliced Almonds, broken up

MAPLE SYRUP GLAZE

1 cup Powdered Sugar

3 Tbsp Maple Syrup

3–5 Tbsp Butter, melted

Dash of Salt

DIRECTIONS

1. Preheat oven to 350 degrees.

2. Butter a 9 inch bundt pan, lightly dust with flour or use non-stick cooking spray.

3. Make the streusel first. In a bowl whisk together the flour, sugar, cinnamon and salt. Cut in the cold butter with a pastry cutter or food processor until the mixture is crumbly or like rough sand. Add in the almonds.

4. Reserve ½ cup of the streusel for the top of the cake. Cut up the apples in small pieces. Mix in with the streusel mixture.

5. In a bowl, add in the flour, salt, baking powder, baking soda and spices. Whisk together until fully mixed.

6. In a mixing bowl, using the flat paddle, beat the butter until smooth. Add in the sugar and continue to beat until smooth and thoroughly combined.

7. Add in the sour cream, pumpkin butter, and vanilla. Mix until combined. Add in eggs, one at a time until just incorporated.

8. Gradually add in the dry ingredients and mix until combined. Slowly add in the apple cider and maple syrup until just blended.

9. Pour half the batter in the baking pan and evenly smooth out the batter. Evenly add in the apple streusel mixture in the middle of the batter.

10. Add the remaining batter on top of the apple streusel mixture evenly spreading the batter over it. Sprinkle the remaining streusel on top of the cake.

11. Bake the coffee cake for about 60–70 minutes until done.

12. While the coffee cake is baking, make the glaze. Melt the butter and add to the maple syrup.

13. In a bowl add in the powdered sugar and salt and stir. Add in the butter-maple syrup mixture and stir until fully combined. Drizzle over the cooled cake and sprinkle with almonds, if desired.

SERVINGS: 4–6

TIME: 1 HOUR 15 MINUTES

DIFFICULTY: INTERMEDIATE

CARROT CAKE so SCRUMPTIOUS

It took me a while to come up with this recipe, because I wanted to recreate one made a long time ago for my daughter, I believe I achieved it with this recipe.

This cake is moist, full of spice and carrots. Traditional cream cheese frosting works well, but I have also used a buttercream frosting. Both taste great on this cake.

Give this cake a bake because it is scrumptious.

" This cake is moist, and full of spice and carrots.

INGREDIENTS

2 ½ cups All Purpose Flour

2 tsp Baking Soda

2 Tbsp Cinnamon

½ tsp Nutmeg

1 tsp Ginger

½ tsp Salt

½ cup Butter,
room temperature

1 cup Sugar

1 cup Brown Sugar,
lightly packed

½ cup Oil (*I use Canola*)

4 Eggs

¾ cup Buttermilk

2 tsp Vanilla

3 cups Carrots, grated

⅔ cups Golden Raisins

CREAM CHEESE FROSTING

1 ½ pkgs Cream Cheese

½ cup Butter, softened

⅓ cup Brown Sugar

½ tsp Vanilla

5–6 cups Powdered Sugar

PECAN TOPPING

1 ½ cups Pecans, chopped

1 Tbsp Butter

Dash of Salt

SERVINGS: 4–6

TIME: 1 HOUR 30 MINUTES

DIFFICULTY: INTERMEDIATE

DIRECTIONS

1. Preheat oven to 375 degrees. Grease and flour two cake pans.

2. In a mixing bowl, cream the butter. Then add in the sugar and mix until light and fluffy. Add in the oil and beat until incorporated. Then add in one egg at a time until incorporated together.

3. In a bowl mix the flour, baking soda, spices and salt. In another bowl add the vanilla to the buttermilk.

4. Alternate adding the flour and buttermilk mixture into the creamed sugar butter mixture. Start with adding one third of the flour to the creamed butter sugar mixture and mix until just combined. Then add in half of the buttermilk mixture and mix and then another third of the flour, the remaining buttermilk and end with the flour. Mix batter until combined.

5. Gently fold in the carrots and raisins.

6. Pour batter evenly into prepared pans. Bake for about 32–40 minutes until the toothpick comes out clean.

7. Cool the cakes for about 30 minutes, then gently remove from pans and rest on a wire rack. Continue to cool completely before frosting.

8. Level the bottom cake layer and if needed, level the top before frosting. Use about ⅔ cup of frosting on the bottom layer. Place the second cake layer on top and finish frosting the cake, starting with the top and then the sides.

CREAM CHEESE FROSTING

1. In a bowl, using a whisk or paddle attachment, add in the first four ingredients and whip until fully combined.

2. Add in one cup of powdered sugar at a time, mixing for about a minute before adding next cup of powdered sugar. Repeat until the frosting is the desired consistency. Frosting should be soft but not too thick. If it's too thick add in about a tsp of milk, if it's too runny add a little powdered sugar.

PECAN TOPPING

1. In a sauté pan, on medium low heat, melt the butter. Add in the pecans and salt and toast until just lightly browned. Scatter the pecans on top and around the bottom edge of the cake, if desired.

Notes

Notes

CHOCOLATE CAKE

I wanted to make a rich, dark, chocolate cake bursting with flavor.

Mayo, coffee, and bittersweet chocolate chips are the key ingredients for this rich, smooth, moist cake.

What better way to start the morning than to have a little slice of chocolate cake?

" This cake uses mayo and coffee creating a nice rich flavor.

INGREDIENTS

1 ½ cups brewed Coffee, hot, non-flavored

1 cup unsweetened Cocoa Powder *(I use special dark)*

3 cups All Purpose Flour

2 tsp Baking Soda

1 tsp Baking Powder

½ tsp Salt

2 ½ cups Sugar

4 large Eggs

1 cup Mayo *(replaces oil, has egg and vinegar)*

1 ½ tsp vanilla

FROSTING

2 cups bittersweet Chocolate Chips

3 ½ Tbsp Light Corn Syrup

4–6 Tbsp Heavy Cream

1 cup Unsalted Butter, softened

½ tsp Vanilla

4–5 cups Powdered Sugar, divided

½ tsp Salt

SERVINGS: 4–6

TIME: 1 HOUR 30 MINUTES

DIFFICULTY: INTERMEDIATE

DIRECTIONS

1. Preheat oven to 350 degrees. Grease and flour two cake pans. *(2 9½ or 3 6½ inch pans)*

2. Whisk together hot coffee and cocoa in a bowl until mixed. Let stand until cooled down to room temperature, about 20–25 minutes.

3. In another bowl, whisked together flour, baking soda, baking powder and ½ tsp salt.

4. In a large bowl combine sugar and eggs. Beat with an electric mixer on medium–low speed until light and fluffy, about 5 minutes.

5. On low speed, mix in mayonnaise and 1½ tsp of vanilla.

6. On low speed, alternate adding flour mixture and coffee mixture to egg sugar mixture starting and ending with flour mixture *(flour, coffee-cocoa, flour, coffee-cocoa, flour)*.

7. Divide batter evenly among prepared pans. Bake until a wooden toothpick or knife inserted in the center comes out with moist crumbs and clean, about 25-30 minutes.

8. Cool cake in pans for about 20 minutes and then remove cake layers from pans and cool completely on racks for another 30 minutes.

FROSTING

1. Place chocolate chips, light corn syrup and 4 Tbsp heavy cream in a microwave bowl. Microwave for about 30 seconds, stir, microwave for another 30 seconds until smooth. Let stand until room temperature.

2. In a bowl, combine butter, ½ tsp salt, 3 cups of powdered sugar and beat on low speed until smooth.

3. Add in chocolate mixture and continue to mix on low speed until smooth.

4. Add in remaining 2 cups of powdered sugar. If needed, add 1 Tbsp heavy cream at a time until you get a spreadable consistency you desire.

5. Place one cake layer on a serving plate, remove any loose crumbs. *If needed, use a bread knife to slice off the crown of the top of the cake to create an equal all around layer.*

6. Spread about 1 cup frosting on top. Add the second layer of cake and spread remaining frosting over the top and sides.

7. Decorate as desired.

CLASSIC CHEESECAKE

I like to make a simple classic cheesecake for Easter. It's been a family tradition that I am continuing with Chris.

I use Greek yogurt instead of sour cream, because it gives it a richer, smoother, creamier texture.

For the crust, I use plain shortbread cookie in place of graham crackers. I think it gives it a mellower flavor, and isn't as dominating as graham crackers can be. I've used half shortbread cookies and half graham crackers, too. Use your imagination to create your perfect crusts from your favorite flavors.

66 My version of a rich and creamy classic cheesecake.

INGREDIENTS

3 8 oz packages Cream Cheese, softened at room temperature

1 cup plain Greek Yogurt
(Sour cream is classic, but I use yogurt because I think yogurt gives it ever-so slightly tang and creaminess)

¼ cup Sour Cream

1 ¼ cup Sugar

2 tsp Vanilla

3 large Eggs, plus 2 Egg Yolks, room temperature

3 Tbsp All Purpose Flour

½ cup Heavy Cream

CRUST

You can use the classic graham cracker, shortbread, or vanilla cookies. All are great, so use whatever you prefer.

2 ½ cups Cookie or Graham Crackers or a blend, crushed into crumbs

1 ¼ Tbsp Sugar

¼ tsp Salt

4 Tbsp Butter, melted

FLAVORINGS / SAUCE

Zest of one Lemon, Juice of ½ Lemon, added to batter

Strawberry

Cherry *(I love)*

Chocolate with Hazelnut

SERVINGS: 8-10

TIME: 2 HOURS 30 MINUTES

DIFFICULTY: INTERMEDIATE

DIRECTIONS

Crust

1. Preheat oven to 425 degrees.

2. Lightly grease a 9 inch springform pan or spray with non-stick cooking spray.

3. Crush graham crackers or cookie crumbs or use a food processor, mix in sugar and salt and blend until fine crumbs.

4. Add melted butter and stir until well combined. Press mixture down firmly into the prepared pan and set aside.

Notes

Continued...

Cheesecake

1. Keep oven at 425 degrees.

2. In a mixer beat soften cream cheese to break it up and smooth, add yogurt and sour cream and continue to beat until smooth and creamy.

3. Add sugar and vanilla and beat until smooth, scraping down the sides and bottom of bowl as needed.

4. Add eggs and egg yolks and beat until mixed in and smooth.

5. Add in flour until just combined.

6. Fold in cream and mix until incorporated into the batter.

7. Pour filling into the prepared crust and spread evenly. Slightly tap springform pan on counter to pop any air bubbles that may have occurred.

8. Wrap the bottom and up the sides slightly with foil. You may need to use several pieces of foil to make sure bottom of pan is completely wrapped. *It's best if one large piece of foil can be used so water doesn't leak in the bottom of the pan and wet the crust.*

9. Place the cheesecake pan into a large baking pan with sides. Fill the pan up with warm-hot water until it comes up the sides slightly. *This is a water bath and will help prevent having cracks in the cheesecake.*

10. Place the pan in the preheated oven and bake cheesecake for 15 minutes. Reduce heat to 325 degrees and continue to bake cheesecake for 1 hour, undisturbed.

11. Turn the oven off and let it rest in the oven for another 30 minutes. The cheesecake will continue to cook and slowly cool down. Test with a toothpick to see if cheesecake is done and not wet.

12. Remove cheesecake from the oven and let it rest on the counter until cooled down, 30 minutes or more.

13. Run a knife around the edge to loosen cheesecake. Remove from the springform pan ring and cover cake with plastic wrap and refrigerate for a couple of hours before serving.

14. Top cheesecake *(optional):*
    - Strawberry or Cherry sauce
    - Chocolate with crushed hazelnuts, optional

Cheesecake, it's been an Easter family tradition, that I am carrying on with Chris.

Notes

COCONUT CAKE with RASPBERRY FILLING

This cake is not just for spring or summer time to make. This is the kind of cake for anytime.

It reminds me of long-time girlfriends sitting around a quaint table catching up on life, or a small dinner party when you want to give a wow factor. You can never go wrong with this cake.

It's light, moist, a little sweet and the tang of the raspberry filling balances it out well.

 I love this cake. It's light, moist, a little sweet, and the tang of the raspberry filling balances it out well.

INGREDIENTS

3 cups Flour, less 6 Tbsp

6 Tbsp Cornstarch

2 tsp Baking Powder

½ tsp Salt

¼ tsp Cream of Tartar

½ tsp Baking Soda

1 cup Butter, room temperature

2 cups Sugar

4 Eggs

1 cup Milk

1 tsp Vanilla

FROSTING

1 ½ cups Butter, at room temperature

7-8 cups Powdered Sugar

⅓ cups Milk

½ tsp Coconut Extract

1 tsp vanilla

1 cup Sweetened Flaked Coconut, for garnish

RASPBERRY FILLING

4 cups Frozen Raspberries

1 cup Sugar

3 Tbsp Cornstarch

2 Tbsp Water

SERVINGS: 6-8

TIME: 1 HOUR

DIFFICULTY: INTERMEDIATE

DIRECTIONS

1. Preheat oven to 350 degrees. Prep two 9 inch round cake pans with butter or shortening and dust with flour.

2. In the bowl of your stand mixer, fitted with the paddle attachment, combine butter and beat until creamy.

3. Add the sugar and beat together on medium speed, until creamy and fluffy. Scrape down the sides as needed.

4. Add eggs, one at a time and beat until fluffy.

5. In a separate bowl, combine the flour, salt, baking powder, baking soda, cream of tartar and cornstarch.

6. Add the vanilla to the milk.

7. Slowly add about ⅓ of the flour mixture into the sugar butter mixture and then add in ½ of the milk, followed by another ⅓ of the flour and the rest of the milk ending with the last ⅓ of flour. Beat until combined and fluffy. *The batter may be a little thicker than usual but this is good.*

8. Immediately divide the batter into equal halves and pour into the prepared cake pans.

9. Bake at 350 degrees for about 25–30 minutes. It's done when an inserted toothpick comes out clean and the cakes are slightly browned, and begin pulling away from the edges of the cake pans.

10. Place the cake pans on a cooling rack and cool for about 10 minutes before removing from the pan. Let cool completely before assembling and frosting the cake.

Continued...

Notes

FILLING

1. Add frozen raspberries to a medium size saucepan on medium heat. Let the raspberries break down slightly.

2. Combine the cornstarch with the sugar and then add to the raspberries.

3. Cook and stir the mixture until it just begins to roll into a slow boil. Slowly stir for about 10–20 minutes until the sauce thickens. If necessary, add a little water if it's too thick.

4. Let the raspberry filling mixture completely cool down before spreading it on the cake.

FROSTING

1. Cream the butter until fluffy.

2. Add the powdered sugar until combined.

3. Slowly add in the milk, vanilla and coconut extract. Beat slowly on low speed and then on medium speed until creamy and fluffy. Add in additional milk if too thick, or additional powdered sugar if too soft.

ASSEMBLING THE CAKE

1. Create a thin frosting ring around the bottom top layer edge of the cake. This will be like a 'guard' to prevent the raspberry filling from sliding off down the cake.

2. Add the raspberry filling to the top of the bottom layer cake. Make sure it is not higher than the frosting ring around the top edge of the bottom layer cake.

3. Place the top layer cake on the bottom and frost the sides of the cake and then the top. Frost how you like—smooth or textured.

4. Add the sweetened coconut flakes to the top and sides, gently pressing into the cake.

" I hope you enjoyed this cake as much as Chris and I did, along with a few friends.

If you want to give a wow factor, you can't go wrong with this cake.

Notes

DARK CHOCOLATE LAVA CAKE

If you love chocolate you'll love this cake. I know, many have made this and I can see why. It is scrumptious, has a rich chocolate taste, and it's easier to make than I expected.

The hardest part of making this cake was melting the chocolate and tempering the eggs. Besides this, it was easier to make than I thought.

Chris loves dark chocolate. I am glad he likes this cake because I will definitely be making it again.

 If you love chocolate you'll love this cake. It has a scrumptious, rich chocolate taste and is easier to make than you think!

INGREDIENTS

4 oz Bittersweet Chocolate, chopped *(100% cocoa)*

4 oz Semi-sweet Chocolate

6 Tbsp Unsalted Butter

3 Eggs, room temperature

3 Egg Yolks, room temperature

1 ½ cups Powdered Sugar

Dash of Salt

½ cup Flour

½ tsp Vanilla

SERVINGS: 4-6

TIME: 45 MINUTES

DIFFICULTY: INTERMEDIATE

DIRECTIONS

1. Preheat oven to 425 degrees..

2. Butter four ramekins, dust with cocoa.

3. In a double boiler, bring water to a low boil.

4. In a separate bowl add the chopped chocolates and butter. Stir frequently as the chocolate melts and is completely smooth. Remove from heat and set aside to cool. May take 15–20 minutes.

5. In a separate bowl, combine the sugar, flour and salt and stir until mixed together.

6. In another bowl *(large enough to use a hand mixer)*, beat the eggs to break up the yolks until thoroughly mixed.

7. With the hand mixer, add the flour mixture to the eggs and mix on low until flour is fully incorporated. Add in the vanilla.

8. Once chocolate has cooled to the touch, add in a couple of tablespoons of the chocolate to the egg and flour mixture and mix to temper the eggs. Continue to slowly add in the remaining chocolate.

9. Divide the chocolate mixture equally among the 4 ramekins. Place the ramekins on a shallow baking pan.

10. Bake for about 10–15 minutes *(depending on your oven)* until the edges of the chocolate cake is firm all around and is slightly away from the edges of the ramekins. If the center of the cake is slightly puffy but still soft and not too jiggly then the cake is done.

11. Remove cakes from the oven and cool.

12. Dust with powdered sugar.

NOTES:

You can use a different combo of chocolates. For example, you can use 60% cocoa or semi-sweet or the combo of both chocolates.

I used powdered sugar because I think it dissolves quicker and easier than granulated sugar and I had a better outcome of the chocolate mixture not tasting a little 'grainy'. However, regular sugar is definitely ok to use.

STRAWBERRY 'SHORTCAKE'

When strawberries are in season, I want to make something different than strawberry shortcake or rhubarb crisp. I want to make a cake, but not frosted, because I want something lighter, that feels like summer or spring time.

This is my version of a strawberry cake. It's a two layered cake, in between a yellow cake and a pound cake with a strawberry whipped cream cheese frosting.

NOTE: This image is from my video. Follow along if you'd like.

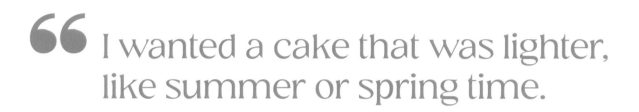

" I wanted a cake that was lighter, like summer or spring time.

INGREDIENTS

1 ½ sticks Unsalted Butter, at room temperature

2 cups Sugar

¼ Sour Cream

4 large Eggs, at room temperature

½ tsp Lemon Zest

1 tsp Vanilla

2 ¼ cups Pastry or Cake Flour
(if using all purpose add ¼ cup corn starch)

1 ½ Tbsp Baking Powder

½ tsp Salt

¾ cup Milk *(add up to ¼ more if batter seems too thick)*

FROSTING

3 cups Heavy Cream

1 cup Powdered Sugar

8 oz Cream Cheese, room temperature

½ tsp Vanilla

2 lbs Strawberries, washed, hulled and sliced in small pieces
Reserve a few whole strawberries to decorate top of cake

SERVINGS: 8-10

TIME: 1 HOUR 20 MINUTES

DIFFICULTY: INTERMEDIATE

DIRECTIONS

1. Preheat oven to 350 degrees. Grease and flour two 8 or 9 inch cake pans.

2. Add flour, salt and baking powder in a bowl mix.

3. Cream the butter and sugar until fluffy, using an electric mixer with the flat attachment.

4. Add sour cream then one egg at a time, lemon zest and vanilla last.

5. Scrape the sides and bottom of bowl and fold into the batter.

6. On low, slowly alternate adding the flour and milk to the creamed butter sugar mix. Don't over mix. Scrape sides and bottom in between adding flour and milk.

7. Evenly pour the batter into the cake pans. Place cake pans in oven on the middle rack and bake for about 25–30 minutes until a knife or toothpick comes out clean.

8. Cool for 10 minutes, then run a knife around the edge of pan to loosen and place on a wire rack. Cool until room temperature.

CREAM CHEESE FROSTING

1. Slice or chop up strawberries in little chunks, reserving a few to decorate the top of the cake. Place in a bowl and set aside.

2. In a mixer, fitted with the whip attachment, pour whipping cream into bowl whip until soft peaks form. *Start on slow then increase speed.*

3. Add ⅓ cup of powdered sugar. Continue whipping until it's slightly stiff. Gently transfer to another bowl.

4. In a mixer bowl with the flat attachment, add cream cheese, remaining powdered sugar and vanilla. Cream until well blended.

5. Drain strawberries if there is a lot of juice, and gently fold in chopped strawberries. Fold in whip cream mixture.

6. Place one cake on a cake stand. Spread about ½ of the frosting mixture on the cake. Place the other cake on top. Spread the remaining frosting on the top of the cake. Decorate cake with reserved whole or halved strawberries.

7. Store cake in the refrigerator until ready to serve.

Notes

Notes

SPICE BUNDT CAKE with MAPLE GLAZE FROSTING

I like spice cake. The warm spices of cinnamon, nutmeg and ginger have this rustic comforting soft delicious taste. It is a cake I like anytime of the year, not just Fall time.

If you're looking for a good piece of sweetness to go with coffee this is the cake. It's good anytime of the day.

I made this cake with unsweetened applesauce for more apple flavor. If you make the cake with buttermilk, it will also add moistness and tenderness.

NOTE: This image is from my video. Follow along if you'd like.

 Warm spices of cinnamon, nutmeg, and ginger have a rustic comforting soft delicious taste.

INGREDIENTS

3 cups Flour

1 ½ Tbsp Baking Powder

1 Tbsp Cornstarch

2 Tbsp Cinnamon

1 ½ tsp Ginger

½ tsp Nutmeg

½ tsp Salt

¾ cup Unsalted Butter

1 ½ cup Sugar

½ cup Brown Sugar

4 Eggs, room temperature

½ cup Oil

2 tsp Vanilla

1 ⅔ cups Applesauce
(or substitute with Buttermilk)

⅓ cup Sour Cream

GLAZE

1 ½ cups Powdered Sugar

3 oz Cream Cheese

½ tsp Vanilla

3 Tbsp Butter,
room temperature

2 Tbsp real Maple Syrup

½ cup Walnuts, toasted and
chopped

SERVINGS: 4-6

TIME: 1 HOUR 15 MINUTES

DIFFICULTY: INTERMEDIATE

DIRECTIONS

1. Preheat oven to 350 degrees. Prep bundt pan by greasing the pan, making sure to grease in the ridges and then lightly flour.

2. Whisk together the flour, baking powder, spices, cornstarch and salt until combined.

3. In a mixer, with the flat paddle, cream the butter until smooth. Add in the sugar and brown sugar and mix well.

4. Add eggs, beating one at a time until combined before adding in the next egg.

5. In a bowl, stir together the applesauce and sour cream *(or buttermilk)*, oil and vanilla until completely mixed.

6. In the bowl with the butter and sugar, alternate adding in the flour and applesauce mixture, ⅓ each, mixing until just combined, after each one and ending with flour. Be sure not to over mix the batter.

7. Pour into the prepared bundt pan. Using a spatula to even out the batter. Gently tap the pan on the counter to 'pop' out any air bubbles.

8. Bake in preheated oven for 45–55 minutes. Check at 45 minutes. If the middle of the cake looks soft then bake for another 5 minutes check with a toothpick or sharp knife and if clean take the cake out of the oven.

9. Let the cake rest for about 15 minutes before using a knife to loosen the cake around the sides and edges. Continue to cool for another 30 minutes before removing the cake.

GLAZE

1. In a bowl, mix together the cream cheese and butter until combined.

2. Add in the powdered sugar and mix until smooth.

3. Add in the vanilla and maple syrup, stir until smooth. Adjust for the consistency by adding in more powdered sugar and/or butter or milk.

4. Drizzle over the cooled cake.

5. Sprinkle with toasted walnuts. *(optional)*

COCONUT CREAM PIE

This pie reminds me of that small-town diner you go visit and their pies are the reason you are there. The combination of creamy smooth custard, coconut flavor, whipped-cream and toasted coconut is scrumptious.

This is an easy pie to make. The hardest part is making sure you temper the eggs right. It sounds more tricky than it is.

I recommend using full fat coconut milk along with half and half. I use half and half instead of regular milk because it makes a richer tasting pie and helps thicken it. You can omit adding coconut into the custard. I prefer it because it gives the pie more coconut flavor, sweetness and texture.

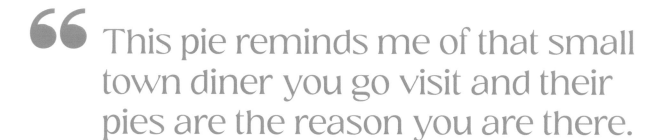

" This pie reminds me of that small town diner you go visit and their pies are the reason you are there.

INGREDIENTS

1 single Pie Crust, either pre-made or your favorite recipe *(check out mine, page 173)*

4 Egg Yolks

¼ cup Cornstarch

1 14 oz can full fat Coconut Milk

1 ¼ cup Half and Half

½ cup Sugar

¼ tsp Salt

1 Tbsp Butter

½ tsp Vanilla

Optional:
½ cup Shredded Coconut

¼–½ tsp Coconut Extract

WHIPPED CREAM

2 cups Heavy Whipping Cream

¼ cup Powdered Sugar

¼ tsp Vanilla

¼ tsp Coconut Extract *(optional)*

GARNISH

Toasted Shredded Coconut

SERVINGS: 6–8

TIME: 6 HOURS

DIFFICULTY: INTERMEDIATE

DIRECTIONS

PIE CRUST

1. Preheat oven to 375 degrees.

2. Prick your piecrust and blind bake until it just begins to turn brown on the edge. *Blind bake means pre-baking your crust.*

3. Place parchment paper on top of the crust, covering the edges as well. Place either pie crust weights or beans on the bottom, enough to cover the bottom and a little up the sides. *You don't want the crust to shrink during this process so the pie weights are important.*

4. Bake for about 10 minutes until the crust just begins to brown. Remove the pie crust from the oven and take out the weights and parchment paper.

5. If you haven't done it already, prick the crust with a fork and bake for about another 5 minutes until the crust is lightly brown. Cool completely before adding the custard to the crust.

Continued...

Notes

FILLING

1. In a small bowl, add the egg yolks and cornstarch and mix until combined.

2. In a saucepan add in the coconut milk, half and half, salt and sugar. Cook on medium–high heat until it comes to a low boil and then reduce to medium low. Add in the butter, coconut extract and vanilla, continue to cook until the sugar has dissolved completely.

3. Take about ¼–⅓ cup of the hot liquid and slowly add to the egg mixture, stirring constantly. Keep stirring until smooth. *Stirring will prevent it from becoming little pieces of scrambled egg.*

4. Add the egg mixture to the hot liquid and keep stirring until the custard has thickened.

5. Once the custard has thickened add to the pie crust. Tap gently on the counter to get out any bubbles that may have formed. Cover with plastic wrap gently pressing down on the custard. *This will help prevent condensation forming.*

6. Refrigerate for at least 3–5 hours before serving.

WHIPPED CREAM

1. In a large mixing bowl add the heavy whipping cream, powdered sugar, vanilla and coconut extract. Mixer on medium-high speed until medium stiff peaks form.

2. Using a spatula spread the whipping cream over the top of the pie, making swirls as you go. Or if you prefer, pipe the cream in dollops to cover the top of the pie.

GARNISH

1. In the oven or in a sauté pan, add the shredded coconut and toast until lightly brown. Sprinkle over the pie.

" From my kitchen to yours, I hope you enjoy this scrumptious Coconut Cream Pie.

Creamy smooth custard, coconut flavor, whipped-cream and toasted coconut combination is scrumptious.

Notes

COUNTRY PEACH PIE

When I first lived on the farm there was a little peach orchard. At first I thought "how are we going to keep this little orchard going?" *(I just had twin boys and had enough to think about and do).* As time went on, we did keep that little orchard going, and it grew until we had a little thriving peach orchard.

Nothing that tastes better than picking a fresh peach off of a tree. It is juicy, sweet and full of peach flavor. The second best thing, besides having your very own tree, is finding fresh peaches at the local farmers market. Thus, came my recipe for peach pie. It speaks of summer and I can't get enough of it.

NOTE: This image is from my video. Follow along if you'd like.

66 Peach pie speaks of summer and I can't get enough of it.

INGREDIENTS

3 ½ lbs ripe Peaches
(about 10–12 medium peaches)

2 Tbsp Lemon Juice

½ cup Sugar, plus a little extra

3 Tbsp Cornstarch

2 tsp Cinnamon

¼ tsp Ginger

1 Egg

1 Tbsp Water

CRUST

3 ½ cups All Purpose Flour

1 ½ ts Salt

1 Tbsp Sugar

12 Tbsp Unsalted Butter

⅓ cup Shortening

12–14 Tbsp very cold Water
(or more if needed)

SERVINGS: 4-6

TIME: 2 HOURS

DIFFICULTY: ADVANCED

DIRECTIONS

PIE CRUST

1. Mix flour, salt, and sugar together. Add butter and pulse with a food processor or use a pastry cutter and mix until flour mixture looks like rough sand.

2. Slowly add the cold water until the flour mixture is wet and comes together.

3. Put dough mixture on a lightly floured surface and form into a ball. Don't overwork the dough because it will have a tendency to be tough and not flaky.

4. Divide the dough in half, wrap in plastic wrap and place in the refrigerator for about 30–45 minutes.

5. Place dough on a lightly floured surface and let rest for about 5 minutes before rolling it out. *This will help the dough to be more manageable to work with.*

6. Roll out dough in two circles that are a little bigger than the pie dish.

Continued...

Notes

FILLING

1. Peel the peaches

   Note: You can use the hot water bath method, but I have to admit I've never done it and found I didn't really need to. I can usually peel the skin off of ripe peaches. However, if your peaches don't peal easily, bring a medium pot of water to a boil. Immerse the peaches in the water for about 20-60 seconds, depending on how ripe the peaches are. Then immediately place peaches in cold to stop the cooking.

2. In a large bowl, slice peaches then add lemon juice.

3. In a separate bowl whisk together sugar, cornstarch, cinnamon and ginger. Add mixture to peaches and gently toss together.

ASSEMBLY

1. Use a rolling pin, roll dough up over pin and then unroll it over the pie dish. Place peaches in the pie crust.

2. Do the same with the pie dough top and place over filling. Trim excess to about ½ inch.

3. Bring the top edge of the pie crust over and under the bottom pie crust and pinch together to seal. Prick the top of the crust to allow steam to release. *For a decorative touch, use some of the leftover dough and a small cookie cutter to cut our different shapes, such as leaves, and place on top of the crust.*

4. In a small bowl whisk together 1 egg and 1 Tbsp of water, creating an egg wash. Using a pastry brush, brush wash over top of pie crust. *This will create a nice golden color on the crust. If you would like, sprinkle a little sugar over the top.*

5. Bake the pie at 425 degrees for 20 minutes.

6. Turn down the heat to 350 degrees and cook for another 30–35 minutes. If the crust begins to brown gently cover the top with foil.

7. Let cool. Serve with ice cream or whipped cream.

Summer + Peaches + Pie = LOVE

Fresh peaches from the local farmers market make the best peach pies!

Notes

KEY LIME PIE

Key Lime Pie reminds me of warm sunshine, palm trees, spring and summer time.

This pie is fresh, tart and sweet and every bite just melts in your mouth.

I must admit, I was a little intimidated making this pie and any pie that has custard. When I was on Celebrity Chopped, I got second place because I couldn't think quick enough on how to make a custard pie or dish.

Making this pie doesn't take a lot of ingredients. Most of the time is baking it, and letting it rest in the refrigerator to set.

 It's fresh, tart and sweet and every bite just melts in your mouth.

INGREDIENTS

2 14 oz cans Condensed Milk

2 Limes, juiced and zested

1 cup Nellie and Joe's
Key Lime Juice *(the best)*

2 Egg Yolks

½ cup Sour Cream

CRUST

1 cup Graham Crackers,
finely crushed

1 cup Shortbread Cookies,
finely crushed

3 Tbsp Sugar

4 Tbsp Butter, melted

TOPPING

2 cups Heavy Whipping
Cream

4 Tbsp Powdered Sugar

2 Limes, zested *(above)*

¼ tsp Vanilla *(optional)*

SERVINGS: 4-6

TIME: 3 HOURS

DIFFICULTY: INTERMEDIATE

Notes

DIRECTIONS

1. Preheat oven to 350 degrees.

2. In a bowl add crushed graham crackers and shortbread and sugar. Whisk together. Add in the butter and mix until the crumbs are wet and come together.

3. In a pie dish, firmly press the crumb mixture on the bottom and up the sides of the dish. Bake for 6–10 minutes until the crust is set.

4. While the crust is baking, in a large bowl whisk together the condensed milk, sour cream and egg yolks until completely mixed together.

5. Add in the juice of the two limes and the key lime juice and whisk together until all the ingredients are mixed together.

6. In the cooled pie crust add the filling. Gently tap the dish on the counter to pop any air bubbles.

7. Bake for about 15–20 minutes until the pie has set and a toothpick comes out clean.

8. Once the pie has cooled refrigerate it for at least 2 hours, if not overnight, to completely set the pie.

9. In a large bowl add the whipping cream, powdered sugar and zest *(and vanilla if adding this in)*. Whip until the cream has thickened enough to decorate the pie.

10. In a piping bag add the whipped cream. Pipe small dollops of cream around the edge of the pie. You can also place a large dollop in the center and add two or three thin slices of lime to decorate. If you have extra zest, sprinkle some all over the pie. *I prefer little dollops of whipping cream around the edge of the pie. This way if someone wants more whip cream you can serve it.*

MINI PECAN PIE TARTS

When I was young, and even into my college years, I never cared for Pecan Pie. In my older adult years, I wanted to give it another try.

I decided to start out small by making mini pecan 'pie' tarts. Let me tell you I love them! They are crunchy with toasted pecans and have just the right amount of sweetness, and the brown sugar gives it a nice rustic, rich flavor.

These are perfect as bite-size sweets for a get-together or party. I made this for a small dinner party and they were a hit. I know I will be making these mini Pecan Pie Tarts again.

 Crunchy toasted pecans with just the right amount of sweetness and a rustic rich flavor.

INGREDIENTS

1 single Pie Crust

1 ½ cups Flour

6 Tbsp Unsalted Butter, cold

¼ cup Shortening

¼ tsp Salt

½ tsp Sugar

6–8 Tbsp Water, cold

FILLING

1 ½ Tbsp Butter, melted

⅓ cup Brown Sugar
(I prefer dark but light works as well)

¼ cup + 1 Tbsp Light Corn Syrup

1 Egg, beaten

½ tsp Vanilla

Dash of Nutmeg

Dash of Cinnamon

⅔ cups Pecans, chopped

SERVINGS: 5-6

TIME: 1 HOUR 30 MINUTES

DIFFICULTY: INTERMEDIATE

DIRECTIONS

PIE CRUST

1. Preheat oven to 350 degrees.

2. Mix all dry ingredients together. Cut in the butter and shortening into the flour mixture until it resembles rough sand.

3. Slowly add in the water until the flour comes together and when pinched it holds together.

4. Refrigerate for about 30 minutes–1 hour.

5. Roll out Pie dough into a circle, about ¼ inch thick. Using a 3 inch cookie cutter cut out pie crusts to fit a mini pie pan. You should be able to get about 24 cutouts.

FILLING

1. In a sauté pan, lightly toast pecans. *This is optional but I prefer the rustic taste of the nuts and this helps take away the 'raw' taste.*

2. In a bowl, mix together all of the ingredients, except the pecans, until completely combined. Fold in the pecans.

3. Using a teaspoon, scoop some pecan pie filling into each mini pie tart to about ½–¾ full. *Be sure not to fill to the top as the filling may overflow and stick to the pan making it harder to loosen each mini pie tart out of the pan.*

4. Cook mini pie tarts for about 15 minutes until set.

5. Cool tarts completely before removing them from the pan. If any filling has overflowed, loosen around the edges as soon as possible with a knife to prevent them sticking to the pan.

Notes

PUFF PASTRY STRAWBERRY TART

A simple and even fancy dessert that's easy to make and for any occasion. It's an easy dessert to have your kids help make.

The combination of the flaky puff pastry, creaminess of mascarpone cheese and sweet strawberries make for a delicious dessert enjoyed by the whole family or your next gathering.

NOTE: This image is from my video. Follow along if you'd like.

 Flaky puff pastry, creamy mascarpone cheese and sweet strawberries make for a delicious dessert.

INGREDIENTS

1 sheet Puff Pastry, thawed

1 Egg

1 tsp Water

¼ cup Sugar

4 cups Strawberries, washed and cut into slices

¼ cup Strawberry Jam

¾ cup White Sugar

4–5 oz Mascarpone Cheese

¼ tsp Pure Vanilla

4 oz Whipped Cream, fresh or pre-made

Mint Leaves, for garnish

Powdered Sugar, topping

SERVINGS: 8

TIME: 40 MINUTES

DIFFICULTY: INTERMEDIATE

DIRECTIONS

1. Preheat oven to 400 degrees.

2. On a parchment lined baking sheet roll out the puff pastry to a large rectangle.

3. In a small bowl, whisk together the egg and water.

4. Use a knife to score a border, about ¾ inch inside from the edge of the puff pastry. Then use a fork to pierce the inside of the tart several times.

5. Brush the pastry with the egg wash along the border of the pastry and try not to let the wash runs down the side. Sprinkle sugar along the border, if desired.

6. Bake for about 20 minutes until a light golden brown. Set aside to cool.

7. While the pastry is baking, in a large bowl, stir together the whipping cream, ½ cup sugar, vanilla and mascarpone cheese.

8. In a separate bowl, mix together the strawberry slices, ¼ cup of sugar and jam.

9. Top the cooled pastry puff with cream mixture, and sliced strawberries then sprinkle with a light dusting of powdered sugar.

10. Serve with a garnish of mint leaves and/or ice cream.

Notes

BLUEBERRY CRUMBLE BARS

These blueberry crumble bars are like having a cookie and a piece of pie at the same time. They are so easy to make and delicious. The blueberries are a burst of sweet and tart and the crumble gives just the right amount of crunch to the soft center.

You can use your favorite fruit, such as strawberries, raspberries, or peaches to substitute for the blueberries.

Visit your local farmers' market for a few pints of blueberries or another fruit to prepare these crumble bars.

66 A burst of sweet and tart with just the right amount of crunch.

CRUMBLE

4 cups Flour

¾ cup Brown Sugar

½ cup Sugar

1 ½ tsp Baking Powder

⅓ tsp Salt

1 ½ cup Cold Butter, cut into small pieces

2 Eggs

FILLING

4 cups Fresh Blueberries

⅓ cup Sugar

4 ½ tsp Cornstarch

1 Lemon, zested

2 Tbsp Lemon Juice

SERVINGS: 4-6

TIME: 1 HOUR 30 MINUTES

DIFFICULTY: INTERMEDIATE

DIRECTIONS

1. Preheat oven to 375 degrees.
2. Lightly grease a 9x13 baking dish

CRUMBLE

1. In a bowl, whisk together the flour, sugars, baking powder and salt.
2. Use a pastry cutter or fork to break up the butter into the flour mixture to resemble rough sand.
3. Press about ½ to ⅔ of the dough into the prepared pan.

BLUEBERRY FILLING

1. In a bowl, whisk together the sugar, cornstarch, lemon zest and juice.
2. Gently fold in the blueberries, coat until mixed altogether.

ASSEMBLE

1. Spread the blueberry mixture evenly over the pressed crumble dough, including some of the excess juice.
2. Add the remaining crumble dough evenly over the blueberry layer while still seeing some of the blueberry filling.
3. Bake for about 45-50 minutes until the blueberry filling is bubbly and the crumble is golden brown.
4. Cool completely before cutting into squares.

Notes

CHOCOLATE CHUNK COOKIES with EVERYTHING but the KITCHEN SINK

I love most every kind of cookie—bar cookies, fruit filled, drop to biscotti, shortbread to the ever wonderful chocolate chip cookie.

I like 'stuff' in my cookies, if the cookie warrants it, and I think this chocolate chunk cookie does.

My biggest question is, do you like soft and chewy or chewy and a little crispy? I have a tendency to bake my cookies a little longer as I think I haven't baked them long enough. Take note that when you take the cookies out they will continue to bake for a minute or two before they cool down.

So, what is Everything But the Kitchen Sink? Pretzels, potato chips, coconut, dried fruit, nuts, peanut butter chips, candy pieces *(Heath or M&M's),* or whatever you may have in your pantry that will elevate this cookie to be even more delicious.

 I like 'stuff' in my cookies, if the cookie warrants it, and I think this chocolate chunk cookie does.

INGREDIENTS

2 cups All Purpose Flour

¼ tsp Salt

1 tsp Baking Soda

⅓ cup Quick Oats (*feel free to toast them a little for a rustic taste*)

1 cup Butter, room temperature

½ cup Sugar

1 cup Brown Sugar

2 Eggs, room temperature

1 tsp Vanilla

½ cup Potato Chips, broken up (*Ruffles are a good option*)

⅓ cup Pretzels, broken up

⅓ cup Coconut, sweetened and shredded

3 4 oz Dark Chocolate Bars, chopped

¼ cup Peanut Butter Chips

¼ cup Heath Bar bits

2 Tbsp Milk, if needed

Walnuts or Pecans, chopped (*Optional*)

SERVINGS: 4-6

TIME: 1 HOUR 30 MINUTES

DIFFICULTY: INTERMEDIATE

DIRECTIONS

1. Preheat oven to 375 degrees.

2. With the paddle attachment, beat butter until smooth and fluffy, then add in the sugars, continue beating until smooth.

3. Add in the eggs one at a time beating after each until just combined, add the vanilla and beat until fluffy.

4. In a separate bowl mix together the flour, quick oats, salt, baking soda and coconut. Slowly add the flour mixture to the butter-sugar mixture and mix until just combined. Try not to over mix the cookie dough.

5. Fold in the broken pretzel pieces, chocolate chunks and peanut butter chips until just combined. Last, gently fold in the potato chips.

6. On a cookie sheet, lined with parchment paper, drop a tablespoon of the cookie dough and if needed, gently press down on top slightly to flatten.

7. Bake for about 8–12 minutes until the edges are lightly brown, taking note that the middle may still be a little soft. If you like a more crispy cookie, bake for about a minute or more longer.

I don't think these cookies will last very long.

Notes

FUDGY BROWNIES with PEANUT BUTTER COOKIE CRUMBLE

I must admit, it's been tough over the years to find a chewy fudgy brownie recipe that isn't overly sweet and cakey, or hard the next day. There'd be times when I made brownies that were so good when I took them out of the oven, but ended up turning dry when they cooled down.

I finally found a brownie recipe that's fudgy and stays chewy, so I just had to share.

I wanted something that reminded me of a peanut butter cup, but not as sweet. I thought wouldn't it be cool if I added Peanut Butter Cookie mix to it as well?

Enjoy my version of a Chewy Fudgy Brownie recipe with a Peanut Butter Cookie Crumble topping.

 I love Peanut Butter Cookies. I wanted something that reminded me of a peanut butter cup, but not as sweet.

INGREDIENTS

8 oz Dark Chocolate, melted

1 ½ cups Sugar

½ cup Brown Sugar

3 Eggs

2 Egg yolks

1 ½ cup Butter

⅓ cup Oil

2 tsp Vanilla

½ tsp Salt

3 cups Flour

¾ cup Unsweetened Cocoa Powder

½ cup Semi-Sweet Chocolate, chopped

PEANUT BUTTER COOKIE CRUMBLE

¾ cup Butter, room temperature

¼ cup Brown Sugar

¾ cup Sugar

½ cup Peanut Butter *(smooth or crunchy)*

1 Egg

1 ½ cup Flour

½ tsp Vanilla

¼ tsp Salt

½ tsp BP

SERVINGS: 4-6

TIME: 1 HOUR

DIFFICULTY: INTERMEDIATE

DIRECTIONS

1. Preheat oven 350 degrees.
2. In a double boiler, melt the 8 oz chocolate. *(see note)*
3. In a large bowl, cream butter. Add in sugars and mix until creamy and fully combined.
4. Add in the eggs and vanilla, mix together until fully incorporated.
5. In a bowl combine the flour, salt and cocoa powder.
6. Chop the semi-sweet chocolate. *(see note)*
7. Mix the dry ingredients into the wet ingredients until combined. Don't over mix the batter.
8. Spread the brownie batter in a 9x13 inch baking dish.

PEANUT BUTTER COOKIE CRUMBLE

1. In a bowl, cream the butter. Then add in the sugars and mix well. Add in the egg and beat well. Add in the vanilla and peanut butter and stir until thoroughly combined.
2. In a bowl, combine flour, salt and baking powder.
3. Add the flour mixture into the wet mixture and mix until combined.
4. Drop peanut butter batter onto the brownie mixture and spread the batter if necessary. It's ok to leave some of the brownie mixture showing. You want each brownie to have a little of the peanut butter cookie crumble on it.
5. Bake Brownie Peanut Butter batter for about 25–30 minutes, depending on your oven and desired doneness. If there are a few crumbs on a toothpick but not gooey, they are done.

NOTES:

If you don't have a double boiler, which I don't, place the chocolate in a glass bowl that fits on top of a saucepan. Fill the pan with water but don't let it touch the bottom of the bowl. With the chocolate in the bowl, bring the water to a slow boil and then down to a low-med simmer, slowly stirring occasionally until chocolate is fully melted. I prefer double boilers rather than the microwave because melting doesn't always work for me as well in a microwave.

I prefer semi-sweet chocolate bars *(like Bakers or Ghirardelli or your favorite preference)* over regular chocolate chips. I find they melt better in the batter. Either chocolate or chips will be fine, though.

GINGER MOLASSES COOKIES

When it comes to warm spices, Fall, and the holidays these cookies are definitely on the top of my list. They have a slight crunch around the edges and a nice soft chew when you bite into them. Perfect with a cup of coffee or a cup of tea or milk.

Be sure to make a double batch as these cookies will not last long.

 When it comes to warm spices, Fall, and the holidays these cookies are definitely on the top of my list.

INGREDIENTS

10 Tbsp Butter, softened

1 cup Brown Sugar, packed

¾ cup Molasses

1 large Egg

1 tsp Vanilla

3 cups Flour

2 tsp Baking Soda

Dash of Salt

2 tsp Ginger

1 ½ Tbsp Cinnamon

1 tsp Cloves

½ tsp Nutmeg

Turbinado Sugar
(for top of cookies)

SERVINGS: 6–8

TIME: 1 HOUR

DIFFICULTY: INTERMEDIATE

DIRECTIONS

1. Preheat oven to 350 degrees.

2. In a small bowl add in the flour, baking soda, salt, ginger, cinnamon, cloves and nutmeg. Whisk together until thoroughly mixed.

3. In a mixing bowl, add the butter and beat until smooth.

4. Add in the brown sugar and continue to mix until smooth. Add in the molasses, vanilla and egg. Beat until combined.

5. Mix in the dry ingredients, a heaping spoonful at a time beating until just slightly mixed in. Continue adding in the dry ingredients, beating until everything is just combined.

6. Gently spoon the dough together, cover with plastic wrap and chill the dough for about 30 minutes. *This will help the dough from being too sticky when forming into balls.*

7. In the meantime, you have time to clean up.

8. Take the chill dough out and with a teaspoon, tablespoon, or cookie scooper *(depending on how big you want the cookies)* form the dough into a ball and place on a parchment lined cookie sheet.

9. Gently press each cookie down slightly with the bottom of a glass or your hand. Sprinkle a little turbinado sugar on top of the cookies, if desired.

10. Bake the cookies for about 6–8 minutes until you see the edges turning slightly brown and the center still slightly soft.

Be sure to share these cookies, they are too good not to.

Notes

STRAWBERRY and CREAM SCONES

Scones are one of my favorite treats to have with coffee in the morning. Depending on the scone I make, I like them for dessert, as well.

The big debate is if a scone is a different version of a biscuit or not. I'll leave that up for debate.

I like a scone that is not too dry and not too wet. I like a scone to be light enough to be crumbly yet not too heavy. A good scone needs to hold up to butter, jam, or another spread.

Here is my version of a light, crumbly scone with strawberries and cream.

 Scones are one of my favorite treats to have with coffee in the morning.

INGREDIENTS

2 ¾ cups Flour

2 Tbsp Sugar

1 Tbsp Baking Powder

½ tsp Baking Soda

¼ tsp Salt

½ cup cold Butter, cut into pieces

1 cup Strawberries, chopped

2 Eggs

¾ cup Heavy Whipping Cream, cold

2 Tbsp Milk

Coarse Sugar

GLAZE

⅔ cups Powdered Sugar

2 Tbsp Cream

SERVINGS: 6-8

TIME: 1 HOUR

DIFFICULTY: INTERMEDIATE

DIRECTIONS

1. Preheat oven to 375 degrees.
2. In a mixing bowl combine flour, sugar, baking powder, baking soda and salt. Stir together until completely combined.
3. Using a pastry cutter, add in butter, cutting it into dry ingredients until crumbly.
4. Add in strawberries and mix into flour mixture.
5. Beat eggs into cream mixture. Gently fold egg mixture into flour mixture until just combined. Be sure not to over mix. *The dough may be shaggy but that's ok. It'll come together as you form it into a disk.*
6. Turn the dough onto a lightly floured surface and gently knead it and fold it into a 1 inch thick circle shape.
7. Cut into about 8 wedges.
8. Place on a parchment lined baking sheet. Brush with milk and sprinkle with coarse sugar.
9. Bake for about 25–30 minutes.
10. In a small bowl mix together powdered sugar and cream.
11. When the scones have cooled down, drizzle glaze over scones and serve.

Notes

SUNSHINE LEMON BARS

I could eat lemon bars anytime of the year and especially when I feel like I want a little sunshine in my day. That's what these bars remind me of...a little sunshine.

I remember making these bars for tea parties with my daughter. I continue to make them today for my family and friends.

These bars are filled with a little tanginess from the lemon and a big kiss of sweetness from the sugar.

Make some today to bring a little sunshine to your kitchen.

NOTE: This image is from my video. Follow along if you'd like.

 I could eat lemon bars anytime of the year, especially when I feel like I want a little sunshine in my day.

INGREDIENTS

3 Tbsp Lemon Zest,
(about 3-4 lemons)

3 cups Sugar

4 Tbsp Flour

8 Eggs, room temperature

1 cup Lemon Juice
(about 4 lemons)

CRUST

2 ½ cups Flour

⅔ cups Powdered Sugar

½ tsp Salt

1 cup Unsalted Butter
softened

1 tsp Vanilla

SERVINGS: 6-8

TIME: 1HOUR 15 MINUTES

DIFFICULTY: INTERMEDIATE

DIRECTIONS

1. Preheat oven to 350 degrees.

2. In a bowl stir together the flour, salt and powdered sugar.

3. Add softened butter and vanilla, mix until dough comes together and is completely combined.

4. In a 9x13 baking dish *(glass preferred)*, gently press dough evenly in the baking dish.

5. Bake cookie dough for about 20 minutes until the dough begins to turn a light golden brown color. Remove from the oven and cool.

6. In the meantime, in a bowl combine the sugar, flour and lemon zest and stir until combined.

7. Add in the eggs and lemon juice, mix well until completely and thoroughly combined.

8. Pour the lemon mixture on top of the crust *(it's ok if still a little warm)*. Bake in the oven for about 25 minutes. They are done when the center is set and it doesn't jiggle.

9. Remove from the oven and cool completely, an 1 hour or more, before cutting into bars. *Hint: cut bars with a sharp knife and wipe clean after each cut.*

10. When bars are cooled, dust with powdered sugar, if desired.

Notes

SNOWBALL COOKIES

This is a traditional cookie I have made during the Christmas holiday since I was a child. I made it with my mom or by myself for years. Then I made it with and for my kids, for Chris and I, and now with and for my grandkids.

This cookie isn't just for the Christmas holiday. It's a good cookie anytime of the year—Valentines Day, spring or summer time, well, anytime is a good time.

It's an easy cookie to make. This is one cookie I don't think you want to substitute out butter in the ingredients. Butter makes this cookie and gives it that rich taste, powdered sugar gives it a little sweetness and nuts give it a little crunch.

This cookie is scrumptious.

 Butter makes this cookie and gives it that rich taste, powdered sugar gives it a little sweetness and nuts give it a little crunch.

INGREDIENTS

2 cups All Purpose Flour

½ cup Powdered Sugar

½-⅔ cups Pecans or Walnuts, finely chopped

¼ tsp Salt

1 cup Butter, softened

Powdered Sugar *(for rolling and dusting cookies in)*

SERVINGS: 6-8

TIME: 1 HOUR 15 MINUTES

DIFFICULTY: INTERMEDIATE

DIRECTIONS

1. Preheat oven to 400 degrees.

2. In a bowl combine the flour, ½ cup powdered sugar, salt and the chopped nuts, mix well.

3. Add the vanilla to the butter and combine the softened butter mixture until completely incorporated in the flour mixture and it begins to come together.

4. Take about a tablespoon of the cookie mixture and roll into a ball. If necessary dust your hands with flour to prevent sticking that may happen.

5. Continue with the rest of the dough and roll into balls.

6. Bake in a preheated oven until set but not browned, for about 12–15 minutes.

7. Cool slightly and then roll cookies in powdered sugar.

8. Cool completely and roll into powdered sugar again.

Enjoy your snowball cookies!

Notes

Amy Roloff is the matriarch of the show Little People, Big World. She recently finished filming the 25th season of the show! Amy is from Michigan and currently lives in Oregon with her husband, Chris, and their rescue dog, Daisy Mae. She enjoys spending time with her 4 children and 8 grandchildren.

Amy loves cooking and baking with her grandkids and teaching them the joys of the kitchen as she learned as a child. She loves babysitting and cheering them on during sports, school events, and other activities.

Amy enjoys the outdoors and taking trips on the motorcycle to the beach and new destinations.She hosts game nights for friends and is always ready for fun game of pickleball. She is often found at her local farmers' market supporting local venders gathering fresh ingredients for her recipes.

AmyRoloffsLittleKitchen.com

Find us on

Notes

Notes

Notes

Notes

Notes

Notes

Notes

Notes